# Railway World

## ANNUAL 1984

£3.95

*Previous page:* **Cumbrian Coast – a diesel multiple-unit forming a Carlisle–Whitehaven train skirts the coast between Parton and Whitehaven, 30 June 1982.** *John Checkley*

*Below:* **Landscape with steam locomotive – LMS '5' 4-6-0 No 5025 running light to Inverness and leaving Kyle on 5 October 1982. Cuillin Hills, Isle of Skye in the background.**
*J. H. Cooper-Smith*

# Railway World

## ANNUAL 1984

Edited by Michael Harris

LONDON

IAN ALLAN LTD

***Cover:* 'West Country' 4-6-2 No 34092 *City of Wells* on the climb from Wennington, near Eldroth on 29 May 1982 with the 'Cumbrian Mountain Pullman'.** *W. A. Sharman*

***Right:* Class 47 Co-Co diesel electric No 47.577 passes Heath Crossing with the 09.35 Saturdays Yarmouth – Cambridge – Liverpool St, 3 July 1982.** *John C. Baker*

First published 1983

ISBN 0 7110 1302 0



Published by Ian Allan Ltd, Shepperton, Surrey; and printed by Ian Allan Printing Ltd at their works at Coombelands in Runnymede, England

# Contents

# Beyond Inverness – to Wick!

## Michael Harris

RAILWAY enthusiasts are an adventurous breed, and there can be few, money permitting, who would baulk at the prospect of reaching the ends of the BR system. Table 239 in the BR timetable is headed 'Inverness, Kyle of Lochalsh, Thurso and Wick'. If you take the 09.35 'Clansman' out of Euston, 10hr 40mins later and after 575 miles travelling (including the run via Birmingham) you are in Inverness. Beyond Inverness, there remains 232 miles of passenger railway to the west and north. It's as far as you can go by BR from London. Who can resist it?

Ever since 1963, the Far North Line and the Dingwall to Kyle of Lochalsh section have been under threat of closure. The Kyle outpost very nearly succumbed in the early 1970s, but if the Invergordon aluminium smelter hadn't become a casualty of worldwide recession and shut up shop in 1981, the railways beyond Inverness might have remained a reasonably safe bet in the future. As it is, with £500,000 worth of rail traffic lost following the demise of the smelter, the going will be tough. However, let's leave speculation to the pundits and take a couple of trips I made in September 1982, hoping that it will be possible to repeat the experience. Part 1 – narrative of a journey to Wick; **Part 2 – photo-tour to Kyle, page 18.**

Trains beyond Inverness usually leave and arrive from their own platforms, Nos 5/6/7 at the bustling station nicely placed at the centre of things in the Highland capital. Bearing a London to Wick BR pass I presented myself to Inspector John Bruce waiting beside Class 37 Co-Co No 37.184 one day in late September. This locomotive had recently joined the allocation at Inverness and looked a trifle battle-scarred, having tried conclusions with something or other at Spean Bridge on the West Highland line. As a newcomer, it was without the tell-tale radio aerial which denotes a locomotive used on the Far North Line. Back in January 1978, heavy snowstorms brought down the overhead railway telephone lines between Lairg and Forsinard. As like for like replacement would be expensive, as well as harking back to the railway past, radio communication was brought in north of Tain as far as Georgemas Junction to provide signalbox to signalbox and train to Inverness Control links in August 1980. With such a far-flung stretch of railway, the new system has given great benefits. Not only is there the chance of constant contact between train and operators, but in case of failures, blockage of the line, or a passenger falling ill on the train, help can be quickly summoned. As in the case of No 37.184, a locomotive without its own transmitter/receiving set carries portable equipment. With that on board, and an Inverness man on driver training, we were all set to leave for the Far North.

Passengers for Wick and Thurso are provided for by separate portions on the Far North trains (all but one designated Class '2', incidentally), detached and attached at Georgemas Junction. Another distinction in these days of uniformity is that the vehicles used on this and the Kyle service are Mark 1 steam-heated stock. On our trip there were three open seconds and a bogie van for Thurso and an RMB (miniature buffet) and brake open second for Wick. The passengers had plenty of room and the 60 people or so contemplating their journey to the north were well-distributed in the five coaches.

Near enough on time, the 11.15 from Inverness eased away from the platform, to take the tablet for the section to Clachnaharry, just across the swing bridge over the Caledonian Canal. Beyond, there was once double track for the next six miles, but this section was singled in 1966. Collecting the tablet for the section to Lentran at Clachnaharry, we were now well and truly on our way. The circuitous course of the line to the Far North is a result of the habitual need for railways to take the easiest possible route. The same was true for the region's roads, until the opening of the Kessock bridge in the summer of 1982 allowed the A9 road to cut across the Black Isle and avoid the detour inland along the shores of the Beauly Firth. The train has no alternative. Locomotives working in the North carry headlamps. To guard against falling rocks, a patrolman was employed to keep a watch on the Kyle line. As an economy measure the patrolman was withdrawn – hence the headlamps. The Class 37s are newcomers to the lines north of Inverness, being introduced in May 1982 on Wick line trains but, at the time of my journey, Class 26s were in charge to Kyle. No 37.184, incidentally, started its BR career in South Wales. The three-axle bogies of

*Above:* **The Wick crew climb aboard Class 26 No 26.038 at Brora. The train is the 11.10 Inverness–Wick/Thurso, and the date, 19 April 1982.**
*Richard Lyndsell*

the Class 37s give a better ride on the curves of the Wick line, so I was told, but No 37.184 was not a particularly comfortable machine.

Along the shores of the Beauly Firth, the line limit is 65 mph and there are stretches of continuously welded track. There was a 20 mph relaying slack after Clunes, a heartening sign that renewal was still in progress, and I was assured that the track on the Wick line was in reasonable shape. Looking ahead, I commented that on this day of veiled sun the combination of blues, purples and browns reflected in the Firth, set off by a sulphurous sky, made the trip a delight. 'When you've played about in the snow', came the reply, 'it loses its attraction'.

We were away from Muir of Ord on time. This station, 13 miles from Inverness, was reopened in October 1976. Happily, vandalism is not a problem in these parts and so the original station remained intact and has been smartly painted in suitable non-corporate identity colours. Alongside the station was the Strathconon postbus, a reminder of the development of these useful services in the north of Scotland. A Class 26 on a freight was waiting at the north end signalbox for the tablet for the section to Lentran.

Dingwall's yard had a few wagons of household coal and we exchanged a handful of passengers and left some newspapers at this busy one-time county town. Now the train started the climb at 1 in 100 to rise alongside the Cromarty Firth. Inspector John Bruce referred to the pride of the local staff, and mentioned that one small link with the past had been severed in the last couple of years, with the retirement of the last driver to have started his career in Highland Railway days. Alness station was reopened in 1973 to serve nearby housing estates, in the days of Invergordon's rapid industry growth. The old station buildings at Alness are boarded up and a Portakabin serves as station facilities. The short, low platform here means that passengers using the station are directed to a specially labelled coach in the train formation.

Approaching Invergordon, Class 37 No 37.262 was standing on a train of alumina and oil tank wagons. Despite the closure of the smelter, alumina was still being loaded at Invergordon for movement by rail to Fort William. The whisky distillery at Invergordon and the oil industry pipe-coating plant were still contributing freight business. At Delny, we came upon the first open crossing with a 25 mph restriction while Nigg, previously the same, now has automatic barriers.

The first sign of the radio communication system came at Fearn with its mast linked by land-line to

Inverness. As the Class 37 rumbled away from Fearn up the 1 in 133, there was a hint of bleaker country and signs of heather and reeds. Across the Dornoch Firth to the east, an RAF jet fighter wheeled away from the bombing range, just to add a modern dimension. At Tain, we exchanged a handful of passengers. As with many other Highland Railway wayside stations, there are two 'signalboxes' here, at the north and south ends of the layout, each with lever frames to control points and signals. The signalling instruments – and now the radio equipment – are in the booking office. Tain is the base for the permanent way department. There were more brilliant colours from wooded hills, heather and sky reflected in the Dornoch Firth, and one or two buzzards overhead as we made good speed towards Ardgay, formerly known as Bonar Bridge. Here, a trio of hikers joined the train. The next stations, Culrain and Invershin, are only 36 chains apart, but separated by the bridge of masonry arches and central girder section which takes the railway across the River Oykell and into the former county of Sutherland. Alongside the River Shin, the real climbing begins with a three-mile slog at 1 in 72 towards Lairg, where there were oil tank wagons in the siding to the distribution depot.

Lairg is just under 67 miles from Inverness. It is the terminus of the Wick line's sole Class '1' train, the Sunday 08.05 from Inverness. This conveys the day's newspapers for the north and is operated for the newspaper proprietors. Passengers are also carried, and from June-September the service is extended to and from Wick and Thurso. From Lairg, the line forges up a 2½-mile climb at 1 in 70 to the 488ft altitude at Lairg summit, still marked by a summit board. Down through Strath Fleet the tempting downgrade is limited by a speed restriction to 45mph. Timekeeping was still exemplary on this journey and we were away from Rogart on time, the orange autumnal bracken on the surrounding craggy hills making a brave sight.

The Mound was formerly the junction for the little Dornoch branch. The branch platform is still intact and the station buildings occupied and neatly kept. Beyond is an open crossing with a 25mph restriction. Golspie, a popular holiday resort, had a household coal wagon in the siding and, as befits the 11.15's role as a mail-carrying train, we offloaded some post. It would be wrong to avoid mention of the third Duke of Sutherland who did so much to develop the railway in the Far North, and the section from Dunrobin (the site of his castle) to just short of Helmsdale was promoted as a private railway. Originally a private station, Dunrobin later became public, but even up in the area there is some doubt when it last received a train, sometime c. 1965. However, the Duke's black and white station building is still neat and tidy. On to Brora, the train runs along the platform formed by a raised

***Left:*** **Class 37 No 37.025 between Rogart and Lairg with the midday Wick/Thurso–Inverness train on 11 August 1982.** *D. M. May*

***Right:*** **Class 26 No 26.029 with the 11.10 Inverness–Wick/Thurso between Lairg and Rogart on 1 June 1981.** *L. A. Nixon*

beach, threading pleasant fields and woods alongside the sea.

Brora is announced by a stop and proceed crossing. On this train, the crews were changed here and Driver/Instructor Peter Keil and Driver A. Clunas made way for Driver Brunton and his secondman, both from Wick. As the passenger trains are steam heated, a two-man crew is of course the rule. In from the north came Class 37 No 37.025 (originally a Great Eastern Line locomotive) at the head of the 11.50 Wick-Inverness, made up of five coaches and a bogie van. The 11.15 down is shown to carry a buffet car to Rogart. This is as unlikely as it seems and in fact marks the point in the journey where the attendant shuts up shop, ready to transfer his attentions to the 11.50 from Wick at Brora.

Problems with the tablet meant that the train was six minutes late away from Brora, and on the next section we snaked along the coastline stretch with speed limits of 45 and 55mph around the curves. Seagulls wheeled around us. Driver Brunton pointed out the oil-drilling rigs 12 miles out at sea, but more picturesque was the beach with pinkish sand and rounded stones. Once an important railway centre, Helmsdale is now rather desolate. There were no passengers on this occasion, and although there were some sorry-looking sidings, not much trace of the former motive power depot.

From Helmsdale, the feeling is of the railway about to embark upon a heroic trek. From Helmsdale to Wick is 35 miles by the A9 road, but to avoid the coastline cliffs the railway builders were forced to strike up the Strath of Kildonan, out over the melancholy land of the Clearances to the boundary between Sutherland and Caithness, otherwise known as the County of the Snowdrifts. With 1,600 amps showing on the clock we did well to maintain 57mph up the broken climb alongside Kildonan Burn on well-maintained track that threads the bleak, open strath. Kildonan is desolate, without buildings but denoted by its railway radio mast. Beyond, on the 1 in 60 gradient, 35-40mph was maintained with 1,900/2,000 amps revealing some doughty work by No 37.184. From within the narrow, wooded valley we looked forward to the hills, civilisation just plausible, thanks to a line of striding power lines. Just after the one-time Borrobol Platform, came the first of the snow fences, a hint of the terrain to come and one which snowed in a Wick line train back in 1978. This led to the West Highland and Far North trains being kitted out with survival rations against any future emergencies.

Kinbrace, with its small post office nearby the station, restores some confidence that *someone* is out here. There is a postbus which runs to Bettyhill and a schoolbus to and from Helmsdale. The grandness of the scenery is undeniable, with distant purple hills mirrored in a couple of lochs near the line. The game is to guess just which is the bleakest

***Right:*** **Georgemas Junction on 23 September 1982, looking south. Class 37 No 37.260 is on the Thurso portion of the 11.15 ex-Inverness.** *Michael Harris*

stretch of railway – my bet is on the four miles of line each side of Forsinard. That station is a traditional crossing place and we left it on time. Snow fences, black peaty earth, heather, grouse and the occasional herd of deer – this sets the scene for the final hurdle on the climb to County March Summit, 708ft up in roadless country. Just beyond this stretch is the cutting into which that Wick line train came up against a 15ft drift. Hereabouts is the spot known somewhat quaintly as the Fairy Hillocks. Altnabreac follows, and then the beginnings of a forestry plantation, one day to break the monotony of these wide-open spaces. Attempts back in the 1950s to exploit the peat reserves came to nothing. Then, Scotscalder and the beginnings of civilisation, but also a wooden fence alongside the facing points formerly at the station – the idea was to protect them from drifting snow.

Civilisation comes back indeed with a vengeance as the train approaches Halkirk: first the girder bridge over the Thurso river, then the road crossing with a 10mph restriction and, to the west, the village. There was a station at Halkirk (closed to passengers in 1960), but the buildings have since disappeared. Despite an apparent case for reopening, Driver Brunton told me that most of the village's inhabitants are commuters to Dounreay or Thurso who would find the train times of little value. If the run from Helmsdale has something of the pioneering spirit, even with diesel power, our driver held my attention with the tale of his favourite run. Two pigeon trains were en route for Wick, an LMS 'Black Five' on each. One failed, and the trains were then combined to make up a 22-van colossus, Helmsdale turning out another '5 as pilot. That meant footplate work at its best, said Driver Brunton!

Georgemas Junction is a remarkable phenomenon. It is here, almost in the middle of nowhere, that the Thurso coaches leave or join the Wick section. The talk is always of the line to *Wick*, but in fact Thurso generates twice the number of passenger journeys. To make matters more interesting, the Thurso line *trails* in at the south end of the station. As we approached Georgemas, a puff of exhaust from the waiting Class 37 (No 37.260) indicated that the Train Game was about to start. The Thurso '37' backed on to the rear of the train, the sections were parted and, after nearly 10 minutes' wait, the two Wick coaches were on their way. Georgemas Junction is a base for the civil engineers and boasts a motor trolley. The last stretch to Wick is something of an anti-climax, cultivated, flat and austere countryside in which the main interest is Loch Watten. On this day, its fishermen were apparently oblivious to a fierce shower. The chance of brisk running is broken by an auto-crossing bringing speed down to 10mph at Watten. Finally, 4¼ hours after leaving Inverness and 729 miles north of London, the train makes a

triumphal approach to Wick station with its all-over roof. The overnight passenger from Euston would have completed a journey spanning nearly 17 hours of travelling and waiting.

Sadly, the days of sheep specials – or racing pigeon trains – are gone, and north of Lairg freight traffic is restricted to household coal and seasonal fertiliser movements. What little there is comes north from Brora on a twice-weekly service to and from Georgemas Junction. There are sights, however, on some Aberdeen-Thurso container traffic which might be worked on an passenger train; maybe even a revival of fish from Wick. The household coal may remain, but it depends on whether the decision is taken instead to feed it into a new coal concentration depot at Inverness.

About 200,000 passenger journeys are made annually on the Wick line, and local and regional authorities and BR are reasonably confident that the 160-odd miles of Far North railway will survive. The Kyle line may be a different matter. The arrival of the Class 37s in 1982 has seen some acceleration of services from their 1970 level. Back in 1947 the Inverness-Wick ride was a weary 6hr ride, but dieselisation and the closure of 20 wayside stations saw that reduced to a best time of 4hrs in 1962. Today's three trains each way make no better time than 4¼ hrs. The easing of some restrictions might allow the odd quarter hour to be lopped off the schedules, but further speeding up is unlikely. The opening of the Kessock road bridge and improvements to the A9 road, combined with the 'deregulation' of road coach services under the 1980 Transport Act, encouraged a Wick-based coach operator to run a 3hr 40min express service to Inverness from the summer of 1982. The fares are extremely competitive, too.

***Above:*** **Class 37 No 37.184, on arrival at Wick with the 11.15 ex-Inverness of 23 September 1982. Its train consists of a brake second and a buffet car.**
*Michael Harris*

Never mind, that detour inland north of Helmsdale and over County March Summit is one of the great railway experiences in the British Isles. Coming back from Wick, again in the cab of No 37.184 – by courtesy of BR Scottish Region – we left the world behind at Scotscalder. The sun behind a heavy, cloudy sky highlighted the heather and moorland grass and in the distance were the Caithness mountains – huge purple-grey shapes dominating the bleak landscape. That's railroading – and with the throaty exhaust of a Class 37 to add character!

# Salute the 40s!

The 'English Electric' 2,000 hp Type 4 1-Co-Co-1 diesel electric locomotives, generally known these days as the Class 40s, have now completed over 25 years service since the first was introduced. But the ranks of this once 200-strong class are thinning rapidly . . .

***Far left:*** **No 40.061 nears the end of its journey with the 08.18 Manchester Piccadilly–Skegness holiday train, passing Thorpe Culvert's somersault distant signal on 28 August 1982.** *B. J. Beer*

***Left:*** **Front-line duty for No 40.034, waiting to leave Holyhead with the 13.05 to Euston on 2 January 1982.** *Michael H. C. Baker*

***Below:*** **A '40' at a London terminus: No 40.028 at the buffer stops, having brought in a special to King's Cross on 13 November 1982.** *Ian Russell*

40 057

***Above left:*** **Rail tour duty: impressively turned out Nos 40.084 and 40.057 accelerate out of Moreton-in-Marsh with an enthusiasts' special, 8 May 1982.** *Peter J. C. Skelton*

***Left:*** **A happy combination of the green-painted No 40.106 and the Steam Locomotive Operators' Association Pullman train comprise the Crewe–Shrewsbury section of the 'Welsh Marches Express', nearing Shrewsbury on 13 March 1982.** *Bill Chapman*

***Above:*** **No 40.138, on its last run before withdrawal, takes the sharp curve through Marsden with a Manchester–Scarborough summer Saturday train on 28 August 1982.** *C. Addis*

***Right:*** **A westbound freight at Hebden Bridge, on the Calder Valley route, behind No 40.046 on 21 April 1982.** *L. A. Nixon*

***Below:*** **Eastbound loaded Sealion engineer's wagons are removed from Helsby sidings by No 40.182 on 18 September 1981.** *Brian Morrison*

*Above:* **On former GWR territory, No 40.126 passes Croes Newydd North Fork Jn with empty tank wagons from Hereford – Ellesmere Port on 7 June 1982.** *A. O. Wynn*

*Left:* **A '40' pilots a Class 86 and a midday Manchester–Euston express through Kidsgrove on 25 April 1982. The power was off and so No 40.184 was promoted to Class '1' duty.** *T. R. Moors*

# Steam to Kyle

On 25 September 1982, the Scottish Steam Railtours Group organised an excursion from Inverness to Kyle of Lochalsh and return. Strathspey Railway-based LMS '5' 4-6-0 No 5025 was the motive power to Kyle. With no turning facilities at Kyle, the '5' had to return tender-first and a Class 37 worked the train back to Inverness. It was one of those rare days in the Highlands, bright, sunny and with exceptional visibility. The result was an occasion to remember . . . .

***Far left:*** **No 5025 waits to take its train into Inverness station, before the outward run.** *John Titlow*

***Left:*** **Passing Achterneed station, on the 1 in 50 climb to Raven's Rock summit.** *John Titlow*

***Below:*** **Before then, No 5025 brings the six coaches of the 'Raven's Rock Express' into Dingwall.** *John Titlow*

LMS

LMS
5025

***Top left:*** **Alongside Lochluichart.** *John Titlow*

***Left:*** **The dramatic backdrop as No 5025 passes Attadale and the passengers see the full glory of Loch Carron.** *John Titlow*

***Top:*** **Approaching Plockton.** *John Titlow*

***Above:*** **Three generations of Kyle line motive power at Kyle of Lochalsh on 25 September 1982. No 26.043 heads the evening service train to Inverness, No 37.184 is at the front of the return 'Raven's Rock Express', ready to depart. No 5025 takes a breather.** *Colin C. Hall*

# Accident at Burnt Oak – 1916

Allan J. Parsons

AT ABOUT 8.25 am on 5 April 1916, the 8.00 am Tunbridge Wells all stations to Brighton train headed by London, Brighton & South Coast Railway 'D1' 0-4-2T engine No 273 left the rails just south of Burnt Oak bridge, turned on its side and completely around. The train was composed of four bogie coaches and two six-wheelers. Only the last vehicle, a six-wheeled milk van, remained on the rails. Injuries were slight considering the extensive damage to the stock and engine.

'D1' tank No 273, formerly named *Dornden,* was considerably damaged having loosened cylinders and bent frames. At the Board of Trade enquiry which followed the accident, it was also revealed that one helical driving wheel spring was found to be fractured; this damage having happened some time prior to the accident. At the time of the incident, the engine had run 1,104,746 miles, with 75,359 miles completed since the last overhaul in March 1913.

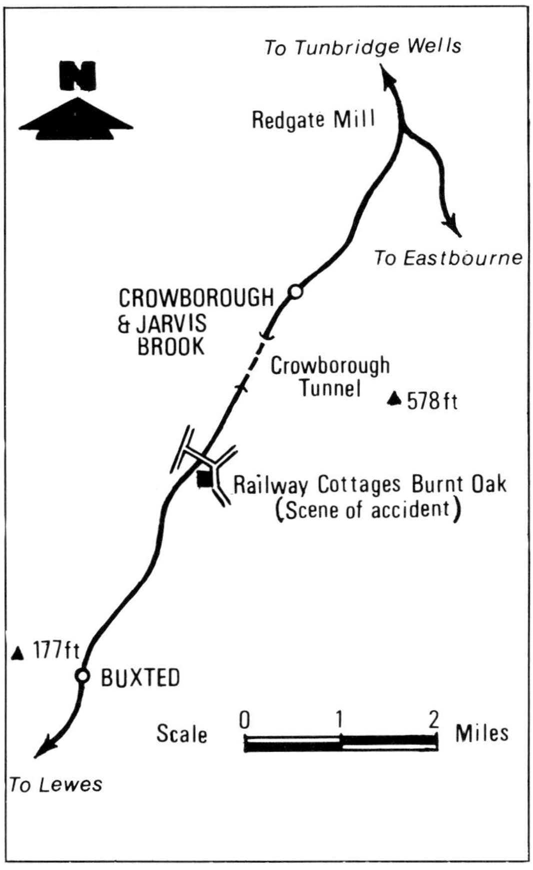


There was conflicting evidence about the cause of the accident but Lt-Colonel P. G. Von Donop, who conducted the enquiry, blamed the poor state of the track. The track was laid with 84 lb/yd, 30 ft rails and the line was on a falling gradient of 1 in 66. Driver John Paige who had been driving the engine for three years stated that there was nothing wrong with the engine. The man in charge of the section of line involved was Assistant Ganger Tidey. He was carrying out maintenance on the track at the time and place of the accident and it was revealed that neither flags nor detonators were used to warn the train. It was also revealed that the train had been delayed for a few minutes as a cow was on the line and the driver was endeavouring to make up time, the train travelling at approximately 45 mph when the leading coupled wheels left the track. The engine continued for seventy yards or so before turning over. The driver was not severely injured, having been thrown head-first into the lineside hedge, but sustained considerable scratches. The fireman was uninjured.

My father was a member of Ganger Tidey's permanent way gang and my parents lived in the Railway Cottages at Burnt Oak beside the place of the accident. I was born in one of the cottages and the photographs illustrating this article were kept by my mother who died recently in her 94th year.

In the area there were considerable army camps during World War 1, and much interest was taken in the accident and the removal of the wreckage; some assistance was rendered by the military.

The Stroudley 'D' tank engines were the next design after the famous 'Terriers' and were altogether much stronger engines and certainly suitable for main line passenger work. The 125 locomotives forming the class were built between 1873 and 1887. Scrapping commenced as long ago as 1903 but the last survived until 1950. No 273 entered service on 29 April 1880 and was scrapped in July 1936.

***Above left:*** **'D1' 0-4-2T No 223 at Brighton Works in Marsh era livery. A sister engine to No 273, it was built in 1885.** *LPC/Ian Allan Library*

***Left:*** **No 273, soon after derailment at Burnt Oak, on 5 April 1916.** *Collection of A. J. Parsons*

***Below:*** **Before re-railing, workers and supervisors pose in front of the luckless No 273.** *Collection of A. J. Parsons*

# Nepal – 'there are no railways there!'

## Derek Cross

'GO TO Nepal! You must be mad. Besides there are no railways there'. This was the reaction of one of my more cynical geological colleagues in New Zealand when I announced that I had been invited to visit Nepal in 1958. Our assistant director said he thought it was a good idea but that I wouldn't be allowed in. At that time, Nepal was closed to outsiders. 'I think I will be OK as I have an invitation from Mr Thapa'. Mr T. had been in New Zealand eighteen months previously studying an irrigation project with which I was involved and his father was something high up in the government in Kathmandu. My boss was nothing if not a tolerant cynic and agreed that such a visit would be a good idea for international understanding. He then added that I would probably have to sleep on the floor of a mud hut; in the event I did so for a couple of days. The next question was how to get there. The local airline in Wellington discovered that it could be done: there was a weekly flight from Patna in Northern India to Kathmandu and, by a lot of hard work, I was assured that I would get a seat, assuming I could get a visa. This took a bit of arranging as postal services to and from Nepal were erratic to say the least and I was told to present myself at the Nepalese consulate in Calcutta, the nearest point for the issue of visas. I wouldn't recommend Calcutta at any time, least of all not in what was the worst heatwave for years. To my surprise, I was met at Calcutta Airport and driven to the Nepalese consulate where I spent a couple of hot, but interesting days.

This was the first surprise. The next was the visa. This was a superb document and fills three pages of my passport from that era and would have put the Magna Carta to shame. The third surprise was Patna which was even hotter than Calcutta, so hot in fact that even the locals were literally dying on their feet. Patna was an important railway junction with lots of interesting things like very elderly 0-4-2 tank engines, but it was far too hot to do the place justice, and I duly reported for my flight to Kathmandu. The aircraft was an Indian Airlines Dakota which caused me the odd qualm as I knew it would have to climb to well over 12,000 ft to clear the Himalayan foothills. With a full load in that heat the Dakota must have been very near its maximum ceiling. Nor was my mind set at rest when one of my fellow-passengers informed me that an aircraft had been lost on that run some months before. Its wreckage had not been found.

I got to Nepal and was much impressed with what I saw in the Kathmandu and Pokara Valleys, both of which are incredibly beautiful, especially in April with the whole range of the snow-covered high Himalayas as a backdrop. The point of my going there was to visit an irrigation project in the Rapti Valley in southern Nepal. To get there involved a long journey by jeep over three mountain passes, the highest of which was nearly 10,000 ft – and this on a road that was still being built. The descent from the final summit was breathtaking, both as regards scenery and hazards. On one length, there were 14 consecutive hair-pin bends! As we dropped down

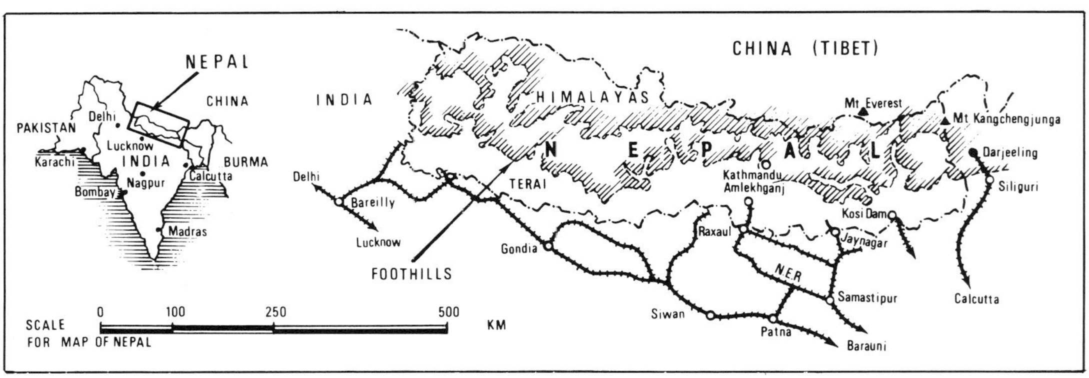

*Left:* **The Nepal Government Railway, to 2ft 6in gauge. Avonside 0-6-2T No 3 *Goraknath* brings a Raxaul–Amelkhganj passenger train through the Terai in April 1958. No 3 was transferred to the Nepal Jaynagar Janakpur Railway in 1982.** *Derek Cross*

*Below:* **NGR No 3 takes water at Birgens on a Raxaul–Amelkhganj passenger train in April 1958.** *Derek Cross*

from the hills, the scene changed and below us lay what was obviously a belt of jungle stretching away to the south before vanishing in the heat haze from the plains. Half-way down I thought I must be suffering from a bad attack of vertigo as I was willing to swear that I saw a plume of steam. I looked again. It *was* a plume of steam and it appeared to be moving through the jungle. Mr Thapa began to laugh and suddenly announced: 'Our railway, pity we have missed the afternoon goods train'. 'But', I spluttered, 'there are no railways in Nepal'. I was sadly misinformed and sure enough an hour or so later we arrived at Amlekhganj where I found a railway yard dozing desertedly in the late afternoon heat. Investigation proved that it was of 2ft 6in gauge and we had indeed missed seeing the last train of the day. Indeed, there were only two, a goods that arrived from Raxaul on the Indian frontier in mid-morning, and a passenger train about lunchtime. The passenger train returned more or less straight-away. The goods spent an hour or two in some dilatory shunting and departed for home at about 14.00. The steam of this working was what I had seen from on high in the hills.

There was no time to investigate matters further as it was considered advisable to reach the irrigation site in the Rapti Valley before dark. This entailed passing through the terai on a series of somewhat rudimentary tracks and it was not considered to be a good place during the hours of darkness. The terai is a strip of jungle varying in width from ten to thirty miles that separates the Himalayan foothills from the northern edge of the great Indian plains. The latter are hot, dry and dusty, but part of the plain is inside the Nepalese border; this was the raison d'être of the irrigation project as given water the plain could be very fertile indeed. The Nepalese were masters at using every cultivable acre they could . . . they had to be, as much of the country is so precipitous that even yaks find it hard to keep their feet. I digress, but claim to be the only railway photographer ever to fall off a yak! Relatively small as Asian jungles go, the terai has a reputation of being the home of many nasty animals, notably snakes, as parts of it are swampy . . . it also contains tigers in considerable numbers. I was to find this out later, having noticed that before we set off for Rapti the driver and gurkha guide both checked that their rifles were loaded and that the passengers knew how to shoot if the occasion arose. Work on the Rapti project proceeded apace, not because I found the floor of a mud-hut uncongenial – as a matter of fact, in that heat mud-huts have a lot to commend them – nor because the Nepalese knew every bit as much about irrigation as I did. To be honest, it was because there was a railway not too far away; what was more a railway that nobody

***Left:*** **No 3 hard at work through the Terai with its Raxaul–Amelkhganj train.**
*Derek Cross*

***Right:*** **NGR, Amlekhganj, April 1958. Garratt No 6 *Sitarama* shunts a goods train while 0-6-2T No 1 heads the daily passenger. The Garratt was subsequently transferred to the NJJR in the late 1960s.** *Derek Cross*

seemed to know existed, and I had every intention of having a look at it. My host connived with the plan and so it was arranged that the twice-weekly trip to Raxaul for camp supplies could be so arranged for me to photograph the daily passenger train.

At this time, as was often the case, the Nepalese and the Indians were not on especially friendly terms so it was decided that I should remain on the Nepalese side of the border. Not that this was any hardship. The start of the 2 ft 6 in gauge Nepalese line was at Raxaul but there was another station at Birjens, two miles away across the border. This was the administration centre of the Nepalese Government Railway and its main, indeed only, depot. I spent some time looking round, in the meantime cursing that I was getting low on film, having blasted off much of my stock on things like Everest and other non-railway matters. Everest will remain, whereas the Nepalese Government railway struck me as being an ephemeral thing. As it happens I was right as the line has been closed. The typical Asian activity that seems to attend the arrival of any train made me realise that the daily passenger train was due so, cameras cocked, I waited to see the fun.

Picture the station at Birjens (sometimes spelt Birganj). It was the typical narrow gauge station the world over, constructed on some Parkinsonian principle that the smaller the gauge the more space a major station needs. Like Swindon it tended to sprawl all over the place, so Parkinson's Law on railway matters may apply to the broad gauge as well! This may have been in my mind at the time, or may have come later but what did arrive *was* Swindonian, an 0-6-2 tank engine appearing out of the heat haze with some fairly respectable looking carriages in a livery that I can only describe as chocolate with a hint of maroon. The livery of the locomotive was a different story altogether, it *was* Swindon: Brunswick green (at least when you looked closely under the grime and dust) with a beautifully polished brass dome and, believe it or not, an equally well-polished copper cap to its chimney. I couldn't believe my eyes . . . it even had a name – *Goraknath*. I gather that this was some Hindu goddess of fertility and not some Nepalese Hall, Grange or Manor, though what the good Gooch would have made of naming engines after godesses of fertility I shudder to think. However, I believe the original Lord of the Isles (human, not locomotive) was not averse to increasing the clans by dalliance with serving wenches, serfs' wives, etc. Closer inspection showed that the home of NGR No 3 was not all that far from Swindon as it had been built by Avonside of Bristol in 1928 for the opening of the Nepalese Government railway.

My utter amazement at this vision was only overcome when my Gurkha driver, who had been guarding my back very closely as we were too near to the Indian border for his liking, and in whose opinion all Indians were most dishonourable, suggested, 'More photos, sahib?' Without a further thought I said, 'Yes, but how?' 'Oh, there is a road, sahib, not good road, not finished, but road all the way to Amlekhganj. Train not very fast and jeep much faster'. To say I was tempted was an understatement. There I was, in a closed country with what amounted to diplomatic status and I was being offered the train chase of a lifetime, and I didn't want to get this charming and friendly man into trouble. I muttered about supplies for the irrigation scheme and got the typical charming, sinister Gurkha smile . . . 'Supplies go in lorry, sahib, I am only escort, perhaps we go to Amlekhganj and see if there is anything for us off the cable lines'. The possibilities were fantastic and as my visa expired in a few days, what the hell if I

were thrown out a day or two early! Added to which the Gurkha had a legitimate excuse. In those days before the road was built through the hills to Kathmandu, there was a cableway over these ferocious mountains that was the main supply route from India to the Nepalese capital. Would that I had more time to look at this as it must have been an incredible feat of engineering; until the road was completed in 1965 it was Kathmandu's main link with the outside world.

As so often in my railway photographic career there was a conflict between decency and deceit, and deceit won the day. I confirmed that my driver would not get into trouble for failing to escort the old Mack truck laden with supplies for the irrigation project. Apparently, the truck driver was his sister's brother's uncle or some tortuous family connection so common in those parts. So I agreed we should return to Rapti the long way round – just in case there was something for Rapti off the cable line. As it happened there were several things. Included was a suggestion that as the monsoon was coming in sooner than expected, once my work at Rapti was completed I should get out from Raxaul rather than return to Kathmandu. It was genuine concern on the part of the Nepalese as in those days getting out of Kathmandu could be tricky in the monsoon season.

The locomotive chase must rank as being among the most unique, if not the greatest. For the first few miles from Birjens the line is relatively level across the dry plain to a small village called, if my memory is correct, Simara. The dirt road followed the railway but the countryside was flat and uninspiring and, with clouds of dust rising in our wake, photography was all but impossible. The line was also fairly level so what photographs I took tended to be at the various village stations, always a source of life and colour, the snag being that I never got the names of half of them. Beyond Simara, the countryside changed dramatically, as did the railway for it was here we entered the dreaded terai. A dirt track that was the start of the construction work for the road that was to kill the railway followed the railway, crossing it at times without warning, much to the peril of the few motorists. My driver who had seen me jump off the jeep for photographs now put his foot down. Handing me a rifle he said I was to sit in the back of the jeep and on *no account* to get off again, at the same time giving the famous, sinister Gurkha grin. The idea of chasing a train clearly appealed to the driver and he set about it with great enthusiasm – much to my alarm and, as I found out later, that of the engine driver. The line starts to climb steeply through the terai, but in the heat there were minimal smoke effects from the locomotive. After a couple of pictures from the back of the jeep, I began to wonder why I could not get off and try another viewpoint. I soon found out. A violent brake application tumbled me into the back of the driver who by this time was yelling 'Rifle, sahib!' Then I saw my one and only wild tiger, a streak of yellow and black darting across the track in our path and obviously disturbed by the approaching train. I was in no position to aim the rifle but would have loved to have shot a tiger and the daily passenger train on one day. After this, I stayed where I had been told. We got to Amlekhganj with a few more photographs in the bag and no further incident.

Maybe I could have done better. There was some compensation for at Amlekhanj was one of the two Nepalese Garratts pottering about in the yard. The 0-6-2T took water, ran round its train and duly departed, once again with passengers festooned on train and locomotive. I had noticed this on the way up but had assumed that it was caused by the sight of a mad photographer chasing the train in a jeep. Not

***Above:* Garratt No 6 at Amelkhganj with a goods train for Raxaul.** *Derek Cross*

so, said my driver. He asked if I had noticed a man sitting on top of the tank of the 0-6-2T. I had, and wondered vaguely why a man in a white dhoti should expose himself to ash and cinders from the chimney. 'He Holy Man, only *very* Holy Men allowed to sit on tank of engine'. 'Why?' I asked, I was given a pitying glance and the incredible, but logical answer: 'Because it is the coolest place on train'. In the heat and humidity of the terai this was probably correct. By now it was obvious that we should be getting back to Rapti, but not before I got a photograph of the Garratt setting out. As usual, my driver seemed to have some distant relation who worked for the railway and so the departure was advanced for our convenience and I was given two pieces of information. The first was infuriating. Had I been there last Tuesday, I would have got some *most* excellent photographs as once a month there was a market at Amlekhanj and a lot of people came up from Raxaul and Birgenj for the market. With the increased load, the Garratt off the goods dropped back to Simara to assist the 0-6-2T on the passenger train up the grades, as steep as 1 in 30 and, I am told, 1 in 24 in parts. That would have been a photograph, tigers or no! I was also told that there was another railway in East Nepal, not that I could have done anything about it as my hard-won visa to that then secret kingdom had expired. Once your visa had run out you were thrown out.

All good things come to an end. With my work at Rapti finished I had to return to New Zealand and since there were mutterings about monsoons I decided to go by rail. At least it would be less hazardous than a Dakota over these mountains. It nearly wasn't. Rapti having been tied up, Mr Thapa had the bright idea that as they had to return to Kathmandu they would drop me off at Amlekhanj to get the train to Raxaul and then on to Calcutta. Like the Highlanders, the Nepalese think than anyone off on a long journey must have a suitable send-off . . . rather on the theory that even if they get there they will probably not get back! In this case it turned out to be a mistake. The driver of 0-6-2T No 3 spotted me and asked through my hosts if I was the man who had taken the photographs some days before. I had to confess I was and was then invited – no, ordered – to join him in the cab for the train was crowded, Nepalese trains tended to be. Like a fool I agreed and we started on our way through the jungle. I was then bidden to drive and while I had driven steam locomotives before, this was something new. The most alarming thing was that I couldn't find the brake. To make matters worse, the driver had a command of English inherited from a Indian Army sergeant-major and it consisted of expletives and very little else. The tigers on the terai may have been frightened that afternoon, but not as frightened as I was when told we had to stop at a small village near Simara. We made it in the end but must have been doing near HST-speeds for Nepalese 2ft 6in gauge by the time we did. I had a very bad few minutes – having found the brake, it wouldn't work!

As it was, my troubles and triumphs were far from finished and I nearly lost all my hard-won photographs. The Indian customs officials must be the most intransigient in the world. At Raxaul, as I was very obviously a stranger coming from Nepal at a time when strangers were not normally allowed there, the local official decided that I was doing something I ought not to have been doing and finally fixed his attention on my cameras. Because these had not been declared on my exit form from Patna before going to Kathmandu he pronounced that I could not bring them back into India. His view was that I must have bought them in Nepal. Who exactly was going to buy a press camera in Nepal – and a sophisticated 35mm model into the bargain – I don't know. I had found to my cost you couldn't even buy film there. The dialogue took time and its outcome was pre-empted by the fortunate arrival of a contractor with earth-moving machinery to bring into Nepal. Whereupon, the officious customs man decided that this was obviously a far larger smuggling racket and so I bolted for the train.

My trip to Nepal in 1958 was a unique experience and I had the greatest pleasure in presenting my doubting colleague with a photograph of a train in a country believed to be without railways. It was one of the unexpected joys of travel in places then off the beaten tourist track, in an age when travel was still adventurous and fun. Even if customs officials were not . . . but then have they ever been?

# Leander

One of the most popular performers on steam main line excursions is LMS 'Jubilee' 4-6-0 No 5690 *Leander*. Upon withdrawal from BR service, it was purchased for scrap by Woodham's Brothers, Barry. Fortunately, it survived to be purchased privately for restoration, and it was brought up to main line running condition at British Rail Engineering Ltd's Derby Locomotive Works in 1973. After seven years' work, it was given a major overhaul at the Bridgnorth locomotive depot of the Severn Valley Railway, and reappeared on the main line in December 1981.

***Leander* thrusts an impressive exhaust into the sky at Stainforth on the climb to Blea Moor with a Leeds–Carlisle excursion, 16 October 1982.** *Paul Claxton*

***Top: Leander*** **was still largely complete when photographed at Woodham's, Barry in 1965.** *Roger Hardingham*

***Above:*** **When first restored, *Leander* was based at the Dinting Railway Centre, and is seen there not long after arrival, in September 1973.** *D. L. Percival*

***Top right:*** **A change of ownership seemed likely to result in the 'Jubilee' being restricted to work on a preserved railway, but new owners Bill Ford and David Clarke decided to base the engine at Steamtown, Carnforth. *Leander* worked from Dinting to Carnforth at the head of an excursion on 24 February 1979, running via Sheffield, Leeds and Skipton, being seen near the last-named.** *D. H. Dyson*

***Right:*** **No 5690 appeared at Rail 150 celebrations in Shildon, and also at Rainhill in 1980, and worked BR's Manchester Victoria–Liverpool 'Steam One-Five-O' trains. Waiting to leave Manchester Victoria, 27 July 1980.** *John Titlow*

5690
L M S

L M S
5690

*Right: Leander's* **reappearance after the 1980/81 overhaul was at the head of a Leicester–Sellafield– Preston charter train which it worked from Sheffield–Leeds– Carnforth–Sellafield. The train was photographed leaving the sad remains of Normanton station on 5 December 1981.**
*John S. Whiteley*

*Below: Leander* **makes a fine sight at Milnsbridge, on the climb to Standedge, with the 6 March 1982 'Trans Pennine Pullman'.** *L. A. Nixon*

MR Compound 4-4-0 No 1000 and 'Jubilee' 4-6-0 No 5690 *Leander* approach York on the East Coast main line south of Skelton Junction with 'The Leander Enterprise' charter train of 20 October 1979.
*Mrs D. A. Robinson*

L M S
5690

L M S

***Above left:*** **Pulling away from the Armathwaite photo-stop of the southbound 'Cumbrian Mountain Pullman' on 23 January 1982.**
*Peter J. C. Skelton*

***Above:*** **A happy combination for working the 'Welsh Marches Pullman' of 13 March 1982. *Leander* has brought the train from Shrewsbury, and has given way to LMS '5' No 5000 which will work the train to Newport and back.**
*Peter J. Green*

***Left:*** **A classic spot for main line steam photography – although loss of the Midland telegraph poles is a pity! *Leander* with the Leeds–Carnforth section of the 'Trans Pennine Pullman' of 12 April 1982. The place? Bell Busk, west of Skipton.** *Dave Hunt*

Twenty years ago steam was rapidly disappearing from East Anglia's railways. Here are two reminders of familiar types in the area.

**'K3' 2-6-0 No 61845 leaves Oakington at the head of a March–Cambridge local in 1959.** *G. D. King*

**'D16/3' 4-4-0 No 62530 on March shed.** *J. Davenport*

**'Jubilee' 4-6-0 No 45562 *Alberta* leaves Bradford Forster Square with a parcels train in the mid-1960s.** *J. S. Whiteley*

***Above:*** **Another '5' and 'Jubilee' combination. *Leander* leads LMS '5' No 5407 on the southbound 'Cumbrian Mountain Pullman' of 31 May 1982. The pair are seen at Cotehill.** *Peter J. Green*

***Below:*** ***Leander*** **leaves Parton, north of Whitehaven, with the return 'Cumbrian Coast Express', formed of the SLOA Pullman set on 30 August 1982.** *John Titlow*

# Train timing

## Peter Semmens

CHARLES Rous-Marten, the 'father' of train timing, died almost 75 years ago, in 1908. He had started the *Railway Magazine's* regular monthly series 'Locomotive Practice and Performance' in 1901, a feature that still appears today under the authorship of the present writer. Indeed, it is the longest-running railway series in the world. Among his timings, Rous-Marten recorded the 100mph sprint of *City of Truro* through Wellington in 1904. In later years there was considerable discussion on the accuracy of his recordings on that occasion. Nowadays, we regularly have speeds of 125mph on our railways, and sustained maxima of 162 across the Channel in France, and it is worth reconsidering the techniques and accuracy of train timing which continues to interest so many railway travellers.

The log of a journey contains two important columns giving the passing times and speeds. The speeds are not recorded directly, but are calculated by dividing a known distance by the time required to cover it. Thus we need to be able to determine distances as well as to measure short intervals of time, equally as accurately. The second of these involves a stop-watch of some sort. A decade ago many wrist watches included such a facility, but they were usually of the stop/start/reset type. It was not possible with these to take a continuous series of timings in the same way as with a split-second chronograph, which lessened the chances of spotting any discrepancies. However, the advent of the electronic watch has altered this, as most of these have a 'lap' facility which permits the re-recording of a series of timings, to a hundredth of a second, although the actual accuracy will not be as high as that in practice, as we will discuss later.

As historic logs were compiled using mechanical watches, and some recorders may still use them, it is worth discussing the accuracy of this form of time-piece.

The hand of a stop-watch moves in a series of jerks and not continuously. The frequency of these jerks is determined by the balance wheel. At each end of its swing it will release the motion to enable it to move on to the next mark, so the hand, therefore, only moves at the end of the period of time registered. Camerer Cuss, the well-known

***Left:*** **The modern railway, with continuously welded track on the fast lines at Burton Coggles, south of Stoke Summit.**

A Crewe Works line-up in the early 1970s with Classes 25, 47 and 40. *D. Birch*

**A Class 253 IC125 speeds across a viaduct between Bodmin Road and Liskeard, forming the 09.25 Paddington–Penzance of 9 January 1981.**
*G. O. Swain*

***Right:*** **The station at Corby Glen closed in 1959, but when this Class 47 was heading a Bradford-King's Cross train in 1969, the signalbox was still in operation.** *R. Elsdon*

***Far right:*** **North Eastern Railway Milepost 162, in section Shaftholme Junction to Moss, East Coast main line.** *R. E. Vincent*

watchmakers, provided me with some information many years ago about the time the hand of the stop-watch actually takes to travel from one mark to the next. This is between 1 and 1½ thousandths of a second in the case of a 1/10th second stop-watch. If the hand of such a watch is arrested mid-way between the marks on the dial, say between 3/10ths (.30) and 4/10ths (.40), it does not indicate that the actual time was 0.35 of a second. The actual time elapsed is 4/10ths minus half the time required for the hand to move – in other words 0.3995 seconds. This is to all intents and purposes the same as 4/10ths of a second and it consequently follows that when the hand is stopped midway between two marks it should always be read to the more advanced of them.

This irregular movement of the hand of a stop-watch means that it is not possible for timings to be more accurate than the time between successive marks on the face. If a train is moving at a speed of 85.2mph, each quarter of a mile is covered in 10.56 seconds. Anyone timing it with a 1/10th second watch will record intervals of $10^{5}/_{10}$ and $10^{6}/_{10}$ seconds, there being on an average slightly more of the latter than the former. If, however, the recorder is only using a 1/5th second watch, there will be a ¼ mile apparently covered in $10^{2}/_{5}$ seconds every 1¼ mile, while the remaining quarters will be covered in $10^{3}/_{5}$ seconds. Consequently, if the speed is calculated to the nearest mph on the single $10^{2}/_{5}$ seconds quarter, it will work out at 87mph against the true figure of 85, both expressed to the nearest whole number. With a digital watch it is, of course, impossible to record times between the smallest consecutive figures on the face, and the electronic logic built into the silicon chip is programmed to carry out the necessary rounding.

While many digital watches indicate times of a hundredth of a second, we must not infer that we can actually record intervals with that degree of accuracy. Those of us who follow modern athletics will perhaps have noted that although records are now quoted to a hundredth of a second, such achievements only count when there are automatic methods of recording available. When the timings are made manually, the greatest accuracy possible is only a tenth of a second. This must apply equally as much to someone recording from a moving train, and there is no point in noting times that are apparently more precise than they actually are. So one rounds the hundredths figure to the nearest tenth. I always put five hundredths 'up', continuing the practice necessary with a mechanical watch.

Because of the limitations of recording times in this way, we have to be aware of the effects on calculated speeds. It is possible to draw up Table 1 showing the limiting speeds in mph for a 1mph level of accuracy in the timings.

**Table I** Maximum speeds at which accuracy of 1mph is obtained.

| | *Timed distance* | | | | |
|---|---|---|---|---|---|
| *Watch calibration* | *¼ mile* | *½ mile* | *¾ mile* | *1 mile* | *1 kilometre* |
| 1/5 | 45 | 65 | 80 | 95 | 75 |
| 1/10 | 65 | 95 | 115 | 130 | 105 |

It will be seen from this table that, even using a 1/10th second stopwatch on *Mallard's* record run down Stoke bank in 1938, a figure that was accurate to less than 1mph in the 126mph maximum could only be calculated by timings over a full mile. The actual record figure was obtained from the dynamometer car roll. This moves proportionally to the distance covered by the car's ninth wheel, and one of the recording pens produces a regular trace-mark on it. By measuring the distance between successive marks, the speed is calculated. This is the exact reverse of our normal amateur techniques, since it uses a variable distance and constant time interval.

So far we have only been considering the errors due to operating the stop-watch, but there is also the question of what is the best form of base-line over which to do the timings. There are three possibilities as far as this country is concerned: mileposts, rail joints and stations. We ought, therefore, to discuss the pros and cons of these various alternatives.

Mileposts are, with minor exceptions, situated every ¼ mile along every line. Indeed, at one time, they were a legal requirement, and the railway could not demand payment for travel over lines without them. Therefore, they ought to form an accurately surveyed baseline, but in practice there are a number of errors, some of which have undoubtedly resulted from a milepost being moved slightly in the course of time. (There even used to be one at Barnard Castle that moved every time a train passed, as it was attached to the level-crossing gates!). Some track realignments have also upset the distances, and the serious student is well-advised to consult Michael Oakley's series of booklets, *Diesel Enthusiast's Pocket Guide*. These give the best available tables of distances I know, and include references to realignments, as well as the truncations that have gone on at some terminal stations where concourses have been enlarged. As far as I am concerned, any timing method that fails to make use of the best baseline immediately becomes second-best, and wherever possible I make use of the mileposts for all my logs.

On those stretches where there is another track between the observer and the mileposts there is little difficulty, from a window seat facing the direction of travel, in sighting each milepost coming up, and then pressing the button when it is 'square' on. In these circumstances, there is always the possibility, of course, that another train may interpose itself at the vital moment, but that is a problem which just has to be endured. There are, however, numerous places where one must record timings from mileposts adjacent to the track on which the recorder is actually travelling. The difficulties presented by this situation can be made worse by poor light, or by the design of posts used by certain of the pre-Grouping companies.

On the majority of my journeys I suffer from the Great Northern Railway version, over much of the distance, whereas the frequenter of the former LNWR West Coast Route is much better-off. Now that locomotives no longer throw sparks, the permanent way gangs are not required to keep the grass short on the sides of cuttings. Consequently, some of the shorter GNR posts are 'lost' in the undergrowth at certain times of the year, and the tops of others are in danger of falling off the rotting wooden posts. Under these conditions, very appreciable errors can creep into the timings, and at times it is all too easy to mistake some other item of lineside 'furniture' for the milepost and stop the watch as that flashes past. Under these circumstances, it is impossible to compile accurate logs without taking a series of timings to determine the speed, since the 'one-off' timing could be wildly out by up to 5, or even 10mph without the observer realising it. The Eastern Region authorities have clearly realised this in recent years and have installed new, larger mileposts on both sides of the East Coast main line. On BR generally, most mileposts are now painted yellow rather than white, as a result of a suggestion made by a railway officer, now retired, when he realised from his own timing activities on the West Coast main line how difficult it was to sight the posts at high speeds.

The vast majority of the British main line permanent way is laid with rails that, even if now welded into longer lengths, were originally 60ft long. There are consequently 22 of these lengths to the ¼-mile, so that if the timing is started at one of the 'ti-ti-tee-tums', and this is counted as '0', it is possible to record the time over a quarter, half or full mile by counting 22, 44 or 88 more respectively, and then stopping the watch. There are, however,

**A Class 108 unit, then recently painted in blue and grey livery, approaches Barrow-in-Furness as the 12.45 Carlisle–Barrow of 27 September 1979.**
*Mrs D. A. Robinson*

**A four-car emu stands at the then recently electrified branch terminus of Braintree, on 12 November 1977.** *G. R. Mortimer*

short lengths of rail from time to time, and points and crossings can also upset the sequence. The most serious problem in using rail-joints, these days, is the use of long welded track. With the BR1 bogies fitted to Mk1 stock, it was usually possible to pick out the passage of the wheelsets over the welds. This has become increasingly difficult with subsequent designs of BR coaching stock, but it is still usually possible to detect the rhythm, even in today's air-conditioned vehicles, if one is near a bogie.

Simple arithmetic will reveal that the number of 60ft rail-joints covered in 41.9secs equals the speed in mph. Consequently, the easiest way of determining speeds when rail-joints are audible is to start the watch at one joint, counting that as '0', and then continuing to count until the watch passes the 42sec mark. If the train is doing 100mph, however, one has to count for $^2/_3$min at a rate of over two per second, and this is a process that is not always without error. While I have often used this method for a quick check, even using a ordinary wrist-watch without a sweep second-hand, it is not really satisfactory as a basis for any accurate recording, because of the absence of any means of detecting errors. As a result, when I am forced to use rail joints, I prefer to count a continuous series of '22s', recording the time at each, so that any irregularities are apparent and subsequently can be discarded. The system thus exactly parallels the one I would employ if the mileposts were visible. Relating the speed recording to an exact point on the track so as to determine the gradient at that point from the published profiles is, of course, nothing like so easy when one is timing from the rail-joints.

There is also the possibility of timing from station to station. Besides making most of the rail-joints virtually inaudible, modernisation has also swept away many of the wayside stations, which, in any case, were rarely less than five miles apart. Their use for timing purposes is limited nowadays, even though traces of many stations can be picked out by an alert observer. Even their signalboxes, which have often outlasted station buildings and station platforms alike, have frequently disappeared. However, there is another drawback to the use of stations as timing points, even those that are still extant. While the station-to-station distances are available from the working timetables to the nearest chain, in the vast majority of cases it is by no means clear from which point on the platform the measurements are taken. For reproducibility, when recording a station passing time, I try to use a passenger overbridge or the station clock, but it is by no means certain that the railway's surveyors used them for their measurements. The North Eastern Railway, however, evidently realised the dilemma that this could cause timing enthusiasts, and marked the datum point on each station with a small metal plate carrying the letters DP either side of a vertical line which was the actual origin for all the measurements. It is interesting to see the various different places on a station where the DP sign used to appear, especially in places where there are staggered platforms. The use of station-to-station timings to determine maximum and minimum speeds is thus very limited.

The recording method I have adopted is based on the foregoing considerations, and has been developed over a number of years. As the train starts out of the station, I set my stop-watch in motion, at the same time noting, *and recording,* the actual time to the nearest second from my wrist-watch. If, in the course of the journey, I should accidentally stop my watch completely, it can then be restarted a whole number of minutes later by reference to the wrist-watch. At all stations, junctions etc, the passing time is noted by stopping the watch using the 'lap' button, and recording the reading to the nearest second. At any of the quarter mileposts where the speed is required, the passing times are recorded, this time to the nearest tenth of a second. In order to save space I use the layout illustrated right, which I usually fill in on specially ruled paper, although it is equally as easy to use it on lined or even a plain sheet. These particular extracts are from a log of a 1970 journey on the 18.00 from King's Cross behind a 'Deltic'.

King's Cross 000 = 17.59.43

| | | | | | |
|---|---|---|---|---|---|
| | | | | Speed (filled in afterwards) | |
| Woolmer Green | 25.03 | | | | |
| Hitchin | 30.38 | | | | |
| 33 | $31.17^4$ | — | — | $44^6$ | 99 |
| 34 | $31.53^6$ | $02^5$ | $11^7$ | $20^7$ | 100 |
| *Check* | | | | | |
| Peterborough | 62.67 | | | | |
| | $72.04^7/13^9/22^7/31^8$ | | | | 100 |
| | $74.47^5/56^5/55^4/14^4$ | | | | 100 |

The figure in the left-hand column in the first two lines under Hitchin is the mileage, and the time at the milepost itself is the first figure entered to the right of it, the superscript figure being the tenths of seconds. When one is travelling away from the mileage zero point, the times at the ¼-mile, ½-mile, and ¾-mile mileposts are entered in order across the line. In the reverse direction, it is the time at the ¾-mile post that follows the whole mile timing.

After Peterborough it became dark on the journey quoted, and I was unable to see the mileposts, so I resorted to timing by counting rail-joints in groups of 22. I entered those times in the log in a similar form to the earlier ones for the mileposts, but in this case I separated them with an oblique stroke to indicate that they were obtained from the rail-joints. Normally, I work out the speed over each ¾-mile and write it in later on the right-hand side of the page. Where the speed over a special section not ending at a ¾-milepost is required, I show the times to which the speed applies by small crosses over the figures. I cannot stress too highly the necessity of recording actual times on which the speeds are based. It is an essential requirement of all scientific work – and this is what train timing is – to record the actual readings made; in this case, the times. Afterwards, as many

***Left:*** **Milepost 35, Scout Green, on the West Coast main line, in 1967. Note the metric distance. Milepost 35 was measured from Lancaster.**

***Right:*** **The switchback gradients of the Salisbury–Exeter line demand careful recording of speeds. Class 50 No. 50.011 at the western end of Buckhorn Weston Tunnel on the 14.20 Exeter St Davids–Waterloo of 25 July 1981.**
*Michael J. Collins*

**On the Glenbrook Vintage Railway, New Zealand, 4-6-4T No 1 makes a fine sight on a passenger train.** *Robin Russell*

In India, a Central Railway broad gauge 'WP1' Pacific No 7656 (built Chittaranjan, 1965), departs from New Delhi, with the 'Taj Express' for Agra, on 29 January 1980. *P. R. Lemmey*

**Table II** Speed/Time Table in Miles/Hour over three-quarters of a mile

*Note:* Inclusion of a speed does not necessarily imply that the timing accuracy is within the limits set by the stop-watch.

| | .0 | .1 | .2 | .3 | .4 | .5 | .6 | .7 | .8 | .9 |
|---|---|---|---|---|---|---|---|---|---|---|
| 20 | 135 | 134 | 134 | 133 | 132 | 132 | 131 | 130 | 130 | 129 |
| 21 | 129 | 128 | 127 | 127 | 126 | 126 | 125 | 124 | 124 | 123 |
| 22 | 123 | 122 | 122 | 121 | 121 | 120 | 119 | 119 | 118 | 118 |
| 23 | 117 | 117 | 116 | 116 | 115 | 115 | 114 | 114 | 113 | 113 |
| 24 | 113 | 112 | 112 | 111 | 111 | 110 | 110 | 109 | 109 | 108 |
| 25 | 108 | 108 | 107 | 107 | 106 | 106 | 105 | 105 | 105 | 104 |
| 26 | 104 | 103 | 103 | 103 | 102 | 102 | 102 | 101 | 101 | 100 |
| 27 | 100 | 100 | 99 | 99 | 99 | 98 | 98 | 97 | 97 | 97 |
| 28 | 96 | 96 | 96 | 95 | 95 | 95 | 94 | 94 | 94 | 93 |
| 29 | 93 | 93 | 92 | 92 | 92 | 92 | 91 | 91 | 91 | 90 |
| 30 | 90 | 90 | 89 | 89 | 89 | 89 | 88 | 88 | 88 | 87 |
| 31 | 87 | 87 | 87 | 86 | 86 | 86 | 85 | 85 | 85 | 85 |
| 32 | 84 | 84 | 84 | 84 | 83 | 83 | 83 | 83 | 82 | 82 |
| 33 | 82 | 82 | 81 | 81 | 81 | 81 | 80 | 80 | 80 | 80 |
| 34 | 79 | 79 | 79 | 79 | 78 | 78 | 78 | 78 | 78 | 77 |
| 35 | 77 | 77 | 77 | 76 | 76 | 76 | 76 | 76 | 75 | 75 |
| 36 | 75 | 75 | 75 | 74 | 74 | 74 | 74 | 74 | 73 | 73 |
| 37 | 73 | 73 | 73 | 72 | 72 | 72 | 72 | 72 | 71 | 71 |
| 38 | 71 | 71 | 71 | 70 | 70 | 70 | 70 | 70 | 70 | 69 |
| 39 | 69 | 69 | 69 | 69 | 69 | 68 | 68 | 68 | 68 | 68 |
| 40 | 68 | 67 | 67 | 67 | 67 | 67 | 67 | 66 | 66 | 66 |
| 41 | 66 | 66 | 66 | 65 | 65 | 65 | 65 | 65 | 65 | 64 |
| 42 | 64 | 64 | 64 | 64 | 64 | 64 | 63 | 63 | 63 | 63 |
| 43 | 63 | 63 | 62 | 62 | 62 | 62 | 62 | 62 | 62 | 62 |
| 44 | 61 | 61 | 61 | 61 | 61 | 61 | 61 | 60 | 60 | 60 |
| 45 | 60 | 60 | 60 | 60 | 59 | 59 | 59 | 59 | 59 | 59 |
| 46 | 59 | 59 | 58 | 58 | 58 | 58 | 58 | 58 | 58 | 58 |
| 47 | 57 | 57 | 57 | 57 | 57 | 57 | 57 | 57 | 56 | 56 |
| 48 | 56 | 56 | 56 | 56 | 56 | 56 | 56 | 55 | 55 | 55 |
| 49 | 55 | 55 | 55 | 55 | 55 | 55 | 54 | 54 | 54 | 54 |
| 50 | 54 | 54 | 54 | 54 | 54 | 53 | 53 | 53 | 53 | 53 |
| 51 | 53 | 53 | 53 | 53 | 53 | 52 | 52 | 52 | 52 | 52 |
| 52 | 52 | 52 | 52 | 52 | 52 | 51 | 51 | 51 | 51 | 51 |
| 53 | 51 | 51 | 51 | 51 | 51 | 50 | 50 | 50 | 50 | 50 |
| 54 | 50 | 50 | 50 | 50 | 50 | 50 | 49 | 49 | 49 | 49 |
| 55 | 49 | 49 | 49 | 49 | 49 | 49 | 49 | 48 | 48 | 48 |
| 56 | 48 | 48 | 48 | 48 | 48 | 48 | 48 | 48 | 48 | 47 |
| 57 | 47 | 47 | 47 | 47 | 47 | 47 | 47 | 47 | 47 | 47 |
| 58 | 47 | 46 | 46 | 46 | 46 | 46 | 46 | 46 | 46 | 46 |
| 59 | 46 | 46 | 46 | 46 | 45 | 45 | 45 | 45 | 45 | 45 |
| 60 | 45 | 45 | 45 | 45 | 45 | 45 | 45 | 44 | 44 | 44 |
| 61 | 44 | 44 | 44 | 44 | 44 | 44 | 44 | 44 | 44 | 44 |
| 62 | 44 | 43 | 43 | 43 | 43 | 43 | 43 | 43 | 43 | 43 |
| 63 | 43 | 43 | 43 | 43 | 43 | 43 | 42 | 42 | 42 | 42 |
| 64 | 42 | 42 | 42 | 42 | 42 | 42 | 42 | 42 | 42 | 42 |
| 65 | 42 | 41 | 41 | 41 | 41 | 41 | 41 | 41 | 41 | 41 |
| 66 | 41 | 41 | 41 | 41 | 41 | 41 | 41 | 40 | 40 | 40 |
| 67 | 40 | 40 | 40 | 40 | 40 | 40 | 40 | 40 | 40 | 40 |
| 68 | 40 | 40 | 40 | 40 | 39 | 39 | 39 | 39 | 39 | 39 |
| 69 | 39 | 39 | 39 | 39 | 39 | 39 | 39 | 39 | 39 | 39 |

**Table III** HST power requirements on level track

| | Horsepower | |
|---|---|---|
| *Speed (mph)* | *Two power cars and seven trailers* | *Two power cars and eight trailers* |
| 5 | 8 | 9 |
| 10 | 18 | 20 |
| 15 | 31 | 34 |
| 20 | 47 | 51 |
| 25 | 66 | 72 |
| 30 | 91 | 99 |
| 35 | 122 | 132 |
| 40 | 160 | 172 |
| 45 | 205 | 221 |
| 50 | 258 | 278 |
| 55 | 321 | 345 |
| 60 | 394 | 422 |
| 65 | 478 | 512 |
| 70 | 573 | 614 |
| 75 | 681 | 729 |
| 80 | 803 | 858 |
| 85 | 939 | 1,003 |
| 90 | 1,090 | 1,164 |
| 95 | 1,257 | 1,341 |
| 100 | 1,441 | 1,537 |
| 105 | 1,643 | 1,751 |
| 110 | 1,864 | 1,985 |
| 115 | 2,103 | 2,240 |
| 120 | 2,363 | 2,516 |
| 125 | 2,644 | 2,814 |
| 130 | 2,948 | 3,136 |

***Below:*** **Plain track marks the site of Steventon station, west of Didcot, as IC125 unit No 253.030 passes at full speed on the 09.06 Paignton–Paddington via Bristol, 4 August 1981.**
*Brian Morrison*

summaries as are wanted may be made, but the complete record is available for checking in case of doubt.

One of the great advantages of this method is that it is immediately possible to calculate the average speed over any distance and in addition, any discrepancies are at once apparent. If, by chance, a signal wire post is timed instead of a milepost, the sudden irregularity in the times will be obvious, and the spurious figures can be discarded.

To convert the milepost timings to speeds, I have tried a number of different methods, including the use of a slide-rule. However, for some time now I have used tables produced by a computer. I have separate ones covering different distances, but have included in this article just the one for ¾-mile. Although the accuracy over such a distance is suspect above 115mph, as already discussed, the table actually goes up to a speed of 135 corresponding to a timing of 20secs for this distance. It will be seen that the whole numbers of seconds between 20 and 69 are printed in order down the left-hand column. As with normal logarithm or other similar mathematical tables, to the right of each are ten figures, being the speeds corresponding to each additional 0.1 of a second.

It is often of interest to use the logs of journeys to compare the relative power outputs on different runs. In recent years, a lot of work has been done in this subject, but in every case it is necessary to estimate the resistance of the train as well as the effect of gravity on rising or falling gradients. Within the space available here, such a subject cannot be discussed at length, but it is worth listing the figures in Table 3, showing the power required to propel '2+7' and '2+8' Inter-City 125 sets on the level at

0-6-0ST No 5 on the North Norfolk Railway (P1970 of 1939) came from NCB Ashington and is seen at the head of an MGNRS special at Sheringham on 3 April 1976. *G. R. Hounsell*

**Wintertime Great Central Railway – LNER 'N2' 0-6-2T No 4744 leaving Rothley for Loughborough on New Year's Day 1979.** *J. H. Cooper-Smith*

the speeds indicated. To allow additionally for the effect of gravity, the following formula is used:

$$\text{Horsepower} = \frac{(\text{Weight of train in tons}) \times (\text{Speed in mph}) \times 5.97}{(\text{Gradient})}$$

(If the gradient is, say, 1 in 120, the figure 120 is used in the formula).

Thus a train weighing 336tons doing 120mph up a gradient of 1 in 200 requires an additional power of

$$\frac{336 \times 120 \times 5.79}{200} = 1{,}204 \text{ horsepower}$$

to maintain this steady speed on the bank compared with on the level. Although all these horsepower figures are expressed to the nearest whole number, the various errors resulting from unknowns, such as wind-speed, make it advisable to quote figures that have been rounded to the nearest 10 or even 50 hp.

When calculating the approximate horsepower, it is important to ensure that one makes allowance for the effects of acceleration and deceleration. Particularly at today's high speeds, decelerations which are very difficult to measure can give falsely high power achievement figures. As an example of this, I have taken some figures from the BTC Performance and Efficiency Test report on the prototype 'Deltic', prepared in September 1956. With a 400-ton train, the locomotive, putting out a maximum brake horsepower from its two diesel engines, maintained a balancing speed of 76mph up a 1 in 200 bank. On the level, with the same train, the power required to maintain this speed was only 1,850 horsepower, 1,400bhp less. Suppose we have a 400-ton train doing 76mph up a 1 in 200 bank, and the driver suddenly reduces the power setting to the 1,850bhp mark. We have removed the power necessary to overcome gravity, so the train will start to decelerate by the effective gravitation component, in other words 32ft per second per second divided by the gradient. This works out as 0.16ft per second per second. Over ¼-mile, therefore, which takes fractionally under 12 seconds to cover at this speed, the velocity would fall off by less than 1½mph, even if we do not allow for the rotational energy in the wheels, axles and other rotating parts of the train. It will be seen, therefore, that even a massive reduction in power results in a deceleration which is undetectable by ordinary stop-watch recordings over a single ¼-mile. If such a train was actually decelerating by no more than 0.013mph over each successive ¼-mile, someone working out the brake horsepower as if the speed were constant would therefore be wrong by something like 100bhp.

These calculations show how it is possible for a high-speed train to 'rush' a bank without any marked falling-off in speed, even though the speed at the top is well above the balancing speed for that gradient. If the power deficiency of a locomotive relative to its load and speed on a particular gradient is constant, the faster it succeeds in approaching the bottom of the bank, the shorter will be the time it takes to climb the incline. The deceleration thus has less time to make itself felt, and so the falling-off in speed as the bank is climbed is lower. A whole article could be written on various aspects of power outputs and, in the space available, this will have to suffice for the present.

**_Below:_ IC125 unit No 254.004 emerges from Stoke Tunnel with the down 'Flying Scotsman' of 24 May 1980. Milepost 101 can just be seen on the down side outside the tunnel portal.** _Brian Morrison_

# Travellers-Fare – the railway refreshment room

H. R. Stones

THE OPENING of the London & Birmingham Railway on 17 September 1838 to Birmingham Curzon Street provided a connection with the Grand Junction Railway for the north-west.

This event heralded the introduction of long-distance rail travel as well as the need to supply food and drink to passengers en route during journeys varying between four and fourteen hours. At that period, the dining car was unknown and at many stations travellers had to rely on the unauthorised bunman who paced the platform with his doubtful confectionery. The advent of the station refreshment room put an end to these activities.

In conjunction with their architects and catering experts the railway companies had to draw on their imagination for the layout of refreshment rooms as even the experience of those who ran inns on the great trunk roads was of little value. At such hostelries customers required quick attention, the speed of the service being dictated by the times taken to change the horses of a stage-coach and this was usually between 20-30 minutes. More significantly, while the road vehicle held no more than about 20 passengers, those descending from a train might number in hundreds. In those days, the bar counter did not exist at inns, the customer calling for his drinks which were brought to him by the landlord or his pot-boys from an enclosed bar and still-room. Meals were served by waiters and waitresses to diners seated in an adjoining coffee room.

So the railways had to find a rapid method of serving refreshments to large trainloads of passengers alighting at specified intermediate stations and junctions during scheduled stops, or while waiting connections – times that varied between ten minutes and an hour respectively. The idea was devised of equipping many of the refreshment rooms with exceptionally long counters at which standing passengers could be served. Labour was plentiful and the numerous staff behind such counters provided a high-speed service. There can be little doubt that the long bar counter now common to hotels and public houses was pioneered by the early railways and subsequently adopted by the catering trade in general.

The first phase of railway catering was covered by refreshment and dining rooms, many in large-scale premises at terminal and important intermediate stations; they were principally staffed by female attendants who mostly lived on the premises. Many of the larger refreshment rooms were practically

***Left:*** **Birmingham Curzon Street goods station and offices (formerly hotel) in 1947.** *BR*

On the Sittingbourne & Kemsley Light Railway, 0-4-2T *Premier* attends to shunting at Sittingbourne on 8 October 1978. *W. B. Hodgson*

**At that stage probably the only surviving Kitson Meyer 0-6-0+0-6-0 in steam in the world, No 61 of the Ferrocarril de Taltal, Chile at the head of a nitrates train in 1971.** *Roy Christian*

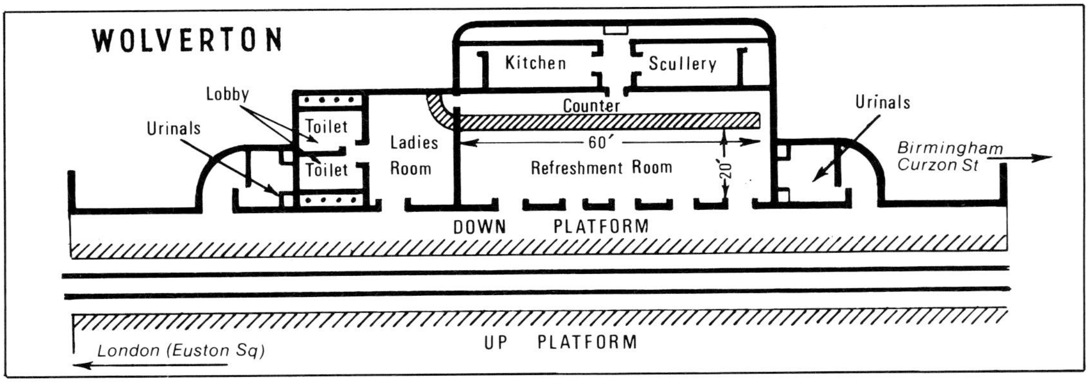


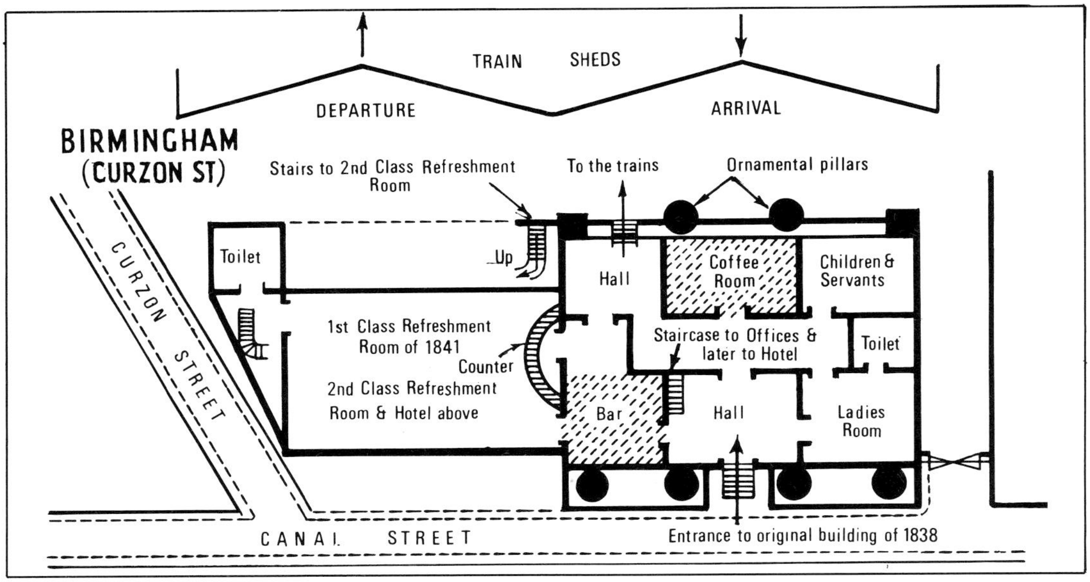


***Top:* Plan of Wolverton refreshment room on the down platform, 1840.**

***Above:* Plan of station buildings and hotel, Birmingham Curzon Street, 1838-41.**

***Right:* South Eastern and Chatham Railway refreshment rooms' tariffs by caterers J. Lyons & Co.** *J. Lyons & Co*

SOUTH EASTERN AND CHATHAM RAILWAY

(London, Chatham, and Dover Section).

ABRIDGED TARIFF OF

BUFFET & TEA ROOMS

. . AT . .

VICTORIA, ST. PAUL'S, AND LUDGATE HILL STATIONS.

And at Margate (West), Ramsgate Harbour, Dover Harbour, Canterbury (East), Herne Bay, Faversham, etc., etc.

Caterers: J. LYONS & Co Ltd.

| | | |
|---|---|---|
| Tea (freshly made for each person) | per cup | 2d |
| Coffee | per cup | 2d |
| Cocoa | per cup | 2d |
| Milk | per glass | 1d |
| Mineral Waters | | 1½d & 3d |
| Scotch Whisky | | 3d & 4d |
| Stout (Reid's) | per glass | 2d |
| Algerian Claret | | 1/3 |
| Graves | | 2/6 |
| Beaune | | 3/- |
| Hennessy's Brandy | | 6d & 1/- |
| Cold Roast Beef | | 6d |
| Ham | | 6d |
| Pork Pie | | 3d |
| Baton (specialty) or Bread | | 1d |
| Buttered Toast | | 2d |

**Confectionery, Tobacco, Cigarettes, and Cigars also at Popular Prices.**

OVER.

SOUTH EASTERN AND CHATHAM RAILWAY.

(London, Chatham, and Dover Section.)

TO TRAVELLERS TO VICTORIA STATION.

Passengers are informed that the temporary Dining Rooms are situate on the Main Line Departure Platform and are under the management of

J. LYONS & Co. Ltd.
the well-known Caterers.

Entrees, Joints, Grill, etc. from 1/-

Cold Meats - - from 10d.

Beverages at Popular Prices.

HIGH-CLASS CUISINE. . . . .

FRENCH & GERMAN SPOKEN.

Also at Ludgate Hill Station.

OVER

self-supporting and maintained kitchen gardens. Pigs fed on kitchen swill were reared on land adjoining the station.

The London & Birmingham Railway was the first to provide adequate refreshments and meals within its station premises at Birmingham Curzon Street. The two-storey station building with Ionic portico designed by Philip Hardwick was completed at the end of 1838. A coffee room with kitchen facilities and an enclosed bar were provided on the ground floor for the convenience of passengers changing to and from trains of the Grand Junction Railway during intervals of ½–1 hour. Three years later, a large refreshment room with dining area for first-class passengers was included on the ground floor of an adjoining hotel extension and this became known as Hardwick's Queens Hotel. A second-class refreshment room was also provided on the floor above. The original station building and hotel annexe were leased to the Railway's subsidiary, the London & Birmingham Railway Hotel Company, which in turn leased them to a private caterer.

The opening of the West Coast, East Coast and Midland long-distance routes to Scotland from the middle of the nineteenth century resulted in longer scheduled stops of between 20-30 minutes at selected intermediate stations such as Preston, York and Normanton. Passengers had to be served en route with adequate meals in dining rooms adjacent to the refreshment rooms.

The historian, F.S. Williams, described a vintage railway station refreshment room of 1852 as follows:

> The long counter with its crystal and plate, mountainous tureens and seething tea and coffee urns, its large plates of pork pies, its strata of sandwiches protected by glass beehives, its masses of cakes and buns for the weaker stomachs of that part of the community who fear to venture on sausage rolls and stout. The milling crowds which descend from a train vociferous in its demand for service, the rapid uncorking of bottles of what is not unappropriately called stout inasmuch as all the persons who are drinking the dark foaming mixture wear great coats with large mufflers round their necks in fact are very stout.

Acworth in *The Railways of Britain* refers to the great range of refreshment rooms which used to occupy nearly all the platform buildings at Normanton and observes:

> Even the famous buffet of Avignon would hardly furnish a dinner of six courses and coffee for half a crown as is done for the Scottish passengers at Normanton.

In comparison with the hustle and bustle of the refreshment rooms, the adjoining dining rooms had a serenity and particular character never surpassed. Thickly carpeted and featuring a bright coal fire in a large open fireplace during winter, they were equipped with gleaming Sheffield plate, engraved cutlery, monogrammed glass and crockery. The tables were covered with spotless white linen and the service predominantly by waitresses provided meals par excellence in true Victorian and Edwardian style.

In the first 25 years or so of their history, most of the station refreshment rooms were leased to individual private caterers. In 1863, a new era commenced when the firm of Spiers & Pond entered the railway catering business in a big way and brought about the gradual demise of the smaller lessees. The long and successful partnership of Felix William Spiers and Christopher Pond began after they had emigrated separately to Australia as young men and met up in the 1850s when Felix Spiers was running the Café de Paris in Melbourne. Together they formed a partnership to supply refreshments to the Melbourne & Ballarat Railway, a contract which was to prove a portent for the future.

Other similar ventures followed. Inspired by their success in Australia, the two restaurateurs decided to return to England and soon secured their first catering contract with the Metropolitan and District Railways in London. Starting with a buffet at Farringdon Street station in 1863, they opened a dozen more on the smoky platforms and concourses of London's sub-surface stations. The following year, they became official caterers to the London Chatham & Dover Railway and inaugurated a refreshment and dining room at Victoria station in London. This was described by *The Standard* as one where 'every convenience for supplying the travellers with chops, steaks, tea and coffee at the shortest possible notice and that, too, in a style fit for a nobleman'. On New Year's Day 1866, Spiers & Pond extended their activities by opening the first Silver Grill restaurant under the arches of the LC&DR at Ludgate Hill station. Later, the firm moved on to secure refreshment room contracts with the larger main line railways, such as the Midland, Great Eastern, North British, Cheshire Lines Committee, Cambrian, Manchester, Sheffield & Lincolnshire, Lancashire & Yorkshire, London & South Western and, in 1899, the South Eastern & Chatham Railway. Christopher Pond died in 1882 and, after Spiers retired in 1904, the firm's association with railway catering was gradually reduced. Its last contracts with the Eastern and Western Divisions of the Southern Railway were transferred to Frederick Hotels Ltd at the end of 1949.

The first long bar counter in the country was installed by the London & Birmingham Railway in one of its refreshment rooms at Wolverton early in 1840. In spite of strictures by the *Punch* of the

**CEGB Donington power station Open Day on 19 April 1980 featured the station's two Robert Stephenson & Hawthornes Ltd 0-4-0STs on demonstration runs. This is No 1 (RSH 7817/54).** *Bryan M. Philpott*

National Coal Board steam at Polkemmet on 5 July 1978. Leading is 0-6-0ST LV8 (AB 1175/08) and behind is 0-6-0T No 8 (AB 1296/12). The pair are working a train between the colliery and the exchange sidings. *A. T. Matthews*

period, Sir Francis Bond Head in his book *Stokers and Pokers* of 1849 gives amusing and favourable accounts of the daily routine junketings at the Wolverton establishment. Situated about halfway between London and Birmingham, Wolverton was selected by the railway as the most appropriate site for its principal locomotive depot and repair shops where engines could be changed and serviced. Advantage could be taken of the scheduled ten-minute stop to provide facilities for passengers to take refreshments. These were first supplied by a local caterer from March 1839 and it is recorded that the first year's takings totalled £3,930 – no mean figure in those days! However, in November 1839 complaints were received about the quality of the food being provided and the caterer was given notice to quit. Two months later, the London & Birmingham Hotel Company took over the catering and a new refreshment room with the first long bar counter – 60 feet in length – was built on the northbound platform. At the end of September 1840, Messrs Dethier and Vantini, lessees of the railway company's Victoria and Euston hotels in London, became the caterers at Wolverton. *Stokers and Pokers* gives an illuminating list of the average annual consumption of food and drink at the Wolverton refreshment rooms. The output included 182,500 Banbury cakes, 56,940 Queen cakes and 29,200 patés, the alcoholic drinks principally comprising 45,000 bottles of stout, 25,690 of ale, 2,390 of brandy and 2,000 of port. Whisky is not mentioned as it was almost unknown in England at the time; even in Scotland its consumption was very limited. A notable personality, Mrs Leonora Hibbert, is described in *Stokers and Pokers* as a 'matron or generalissima' and she was in charge of the rooms for about eleven years. Her name became synonymous with Wolverton and later with Holyhead, to which port she was promoted to take over new refreshment and dining rooms catering for increasing passenger traffic to and from Ireland. Her transfer even received publicity in *Herapath's Journal* of 26 April 1851!

Another early station refreshment room attracting much publicity in the press was at Swindon on the Great Western Railway. Here, as at Wolverton, engines were changed and advantage was taken of the stop to provide refreshments. In 1841, a contract was drawn up with J. & C. Rigby of London to construct station buildings with refreshment rooms at Swindon, but free of all expense to the railway company. On completion, the builders undertook to maintain the premises in consideration of a lease of the refreshment rooms to them for 99 years from Christmas 1841, at a peppercorn rent of one penny a year. To ensure remunerative profits for J. & C. Rigby in return for

***Left:*** **Railway dining room, c 1920.** *BR*

their outlay in carrying out the construction, the GWR agreed to stop all trains at Swindon for ten minutes so that passengers could take refreshments. At the same time, the GWR undertook not to set up any rival stopping place between London and Bristol which might prejudice the receipts at Swindon. The permanent premises opened on 14 July 1842 and consisted of two three-storey buildings with a total floor space of 37,740 sq ft on either side of the main line. Unlike the layout at Wolverton, the ground floor of each building was wholly occupied by a large refreshment room divided by columns into first- and second-class sections with an oval counter in the middle for the sale of food and drink. Catering at Swindon by a sequence of contractors proved unsatisfactory for many years. The famous Isambard Kingdom Brunel was compelled to complain about the coffee served in 1842. It was not until 1895 that the GWR was able to purchase back the lease at a cost of no less than £100,000. An intolerable situation was terminated after more than half a century.

With the introduction of the dining car in 1879, the function of the station refreshment room changed from universal catering to providing travellers with sustenance before or on completion of a journey. Nevertheless, many passengers could not afford dining car meals and still relied on the refreshment rooms, many of which also supplied the more economic and popular portable luncheon basket innovated by Spiers & Pond in 1871.

Other firms followed in the wake of Spiers & Pond such as J. Lyons & Co who were caterers to the London Chatham & Dover section of the SE & CR from 1905 to 1924. Brown & Wesley leased most of the refreshment rooms on the GWR between London and Birkenhead and in the West Midlands until 1895. In that year, the GWR, following the example of the Midland, LNWR and some of the other railways, decided to take over its own catering arrangements. J. Bertram & Co had a contract with the London, Brighton and South Coast Railway (later the Central Division of the Southern Railway) from the turn of the century until the end of 1951.

In conclusion, the writer is indebted to Mr E.H. Fowkes, Archivist of the former British Transport Historical Records Office in London, for permission to consult relevant records, the Express Dairy Company for information concerning Messrs Spiers & Pond and to J. Lyons & Co and others for invaluable help in the preparation of this article.

**The long bar updated in this 1957 modernisation of Southend on Sea Central station refreshment/waiting room.** *BR*

One notable charter train of recent years was the Travellers-Fare 'Centenary Express', seen near Church Stretton behind *King George V* on 15 September 1979. *C. F. D. Whetmath*

# The railways of Majorca


## Giles Barnabe


TO THE average holidaymaker, or even railfan, the name of Majorca hardly seems to be of railway interest. But, for those who are willing to leave the beaches and organised sightseeing tours, and venture out by hired car or even bicycle, the island's railway system has a lot to offer. True, the system is shrinking fast and in some places resembles nothing so much as a narrow gauge version of British Rail with passenger-only services and all but essential track removed. Sometimes advertised train services turn out to be worked by buses – this, too, is not an unknown feature of rural byways in Britain. One main difference, however, is that where a section of line has been abandoned it suffers little vandalism, and if one is prepared to negotiate the weeds and brambles, the visitor can gain an almost complete idea of the island's railway heyday.

Railway history on the island begins in the early 1870s when various schemes were planned. At that time, the roads were merely earth and stone tracks, most goods were moved by mule power, and the average journey between one town and another took a full day. So it is easy to appreciate the benefits brought by railway construction. In fact, the £88,000 capital stock (at the contemporary Victorian exchange rate) for the original line was all subscribed locally, although an English consortium, the Majorca Railway Company, built the line. This was most probably the main factor in the chosen gauge being 3ft, rather than one metre. At about this time in Great Britain the Isle of Man Railway, the Ravenglass and Eskdale, and the first of the Irish lines were all being built to 3ft gauge.

The course of the line from Palma ran roughly north-east to the town of Inca and involved a climb of about 500ft. However, few large-scale engineering works were required and the railway ran unfenced through fields and farmyards. The steepest gradient was 1 in 67 and the sharpest curve had a radius of 228 yards. For the opening of the line, Nasmyth, Wilson & Co of Manchester supplied three 4-4-0Ts, as well as two 0-6-0Ts for shunting and goods work. Brown, Marshall of Birmingham supplied four-wheeled passenger coaches fitted with a double roof to protect the travellers from the heat of the sun. Matching 'birdcage' brake vans were also provided. Centre buffer/couplings were used with safety chains, although screw couplings were later added to the passenger stock, along with vacuum brakes. The locomotives were fitted only with rear end brake pipes and, until the 1920s, sported cowcatchers, so turntables were needed at the termini.

The opening day was 24 February 1875 and the ceremonies must have been a colourful spectacle. The usual triumphal arches had been erected at the Palma terminus, and before the train could depart it was blessed at an open air service held on the platform. Some local farmers doubted that the train would move at all. They reasoned that their kitchen fire stayed where it was; if the locomotive should move, surely the wheels concealed the mules inside! However, the inaugural run duly took place, covering the 18 miles to Inca in 64 minutes. There, the town was decorated with myrtle boughs and flower-covered displays of agricultural tools. After another church service, and the inevitable luncheon and speeches, the special train returned to Palma where less important VIPs were impatiently waiting to board the second train.

Railway travel soon became accepted, and the various stations became the social centres of the towns where inhabitants gathered to talk and watch the trains come and go. Some examples of the fares between Palma and Inca in the early days were: first-class 1/6d (7½p), and second class 1/- (5p). In the first month the line carried 40,000 passengers.

The building costs were approximately £6,000 a mile, and the various stations were let out as individual contracts to local builders. Thus, while there is a fairly standard design, all the stations are subtly different. The normal type consists of a two-storey structure with a waiting room/booking hall with high ceilings. Upstairs is the stationmaster's living accommodation. Further along the platform is the usual outbuilding labled Hombres/Senoras, while the more important stations have a goods shed with a wide roof that overhangs the adjacent track and loading bay. Another pleasant feature was the planting of trees to shade the platforms, a long-sighted provision in those early days.

Shortly after the opening of the line, the British company merged with the Spanish-owned Majorca Central and South Eastern Railway Company which had been planning other lines in the island. Together they became the Compania de los Ferrocarriles de Mallorca, or Majorca Railways. Shortly afterwards, in 1878, the line was extended from Inca to serve the agricultural area in the north of the island, with a new terminus at La Puebla. Next came a line from Empalme station near Inca, running south-east via Sineu and Petra to Manacor, which was reached in 1879. Other lines were quickly added to Alaro (1881), to Felanitx (1897), and to Santany (1917).

All these extensions resulted in an appropriate increase in the rolling stock. In 1887, two 4-6-0Ts were introduced to work the trains as far as Inca, and it became the practice to run the La Puebla and Manacor trains together, to be divided into separate trains at Inca. This method of working was evidently a success as two more of the larger engines arrived in 1891. In the early 20th century, the railway workshops at Palma were building locomotives, as well as dealing with repairs, and the first project was to construct two more 4-4-0Ts. The steam locomotive livery was green and the engines carried numbers as well as being named after towns along the railway. Passenger stock was varnished wood or painted brown. After World War 1, the British influence declined, and the next batch of new locomotives were of Spanish manufacture, being supplied in 1917 for the Santany branch.

The 1920s and 1930s were a prosperous time for the Majorca Railways. Yet more mileage was added in 1921, in the form of eighteen twisting miles of route north of Manacor to reach the town of Arta – 58½ miles from Palma, with a journey time of 2½ hours. The basic service was three round trips daily on each line. This led to the doubling of the Inca – Palma portion of the railway in 1931 as it carried the bulk of the services. Bogie carriages with side corridors appeared in 1930, along with some powerful 2-6-2Ts from Babcock, Wilcox of Bilbao. These could run from Palma to Manacor without stopping to take water. Other lines were planned in this period: a branch from San Miguel to the Caves of Drach near Porto Cristo, and an extension of the La Puebla branch to reach the developing port of Alcudia on the north-east coast. As it happened neither scheme was realised, although both might have provided considerable traffic, in view of the outbreak of the Spanish Civil War.

Unlike the Irish 'Troubles', the Civil War did not cause any appreciable damage to the railway. The result was more insidious as there was an industrial

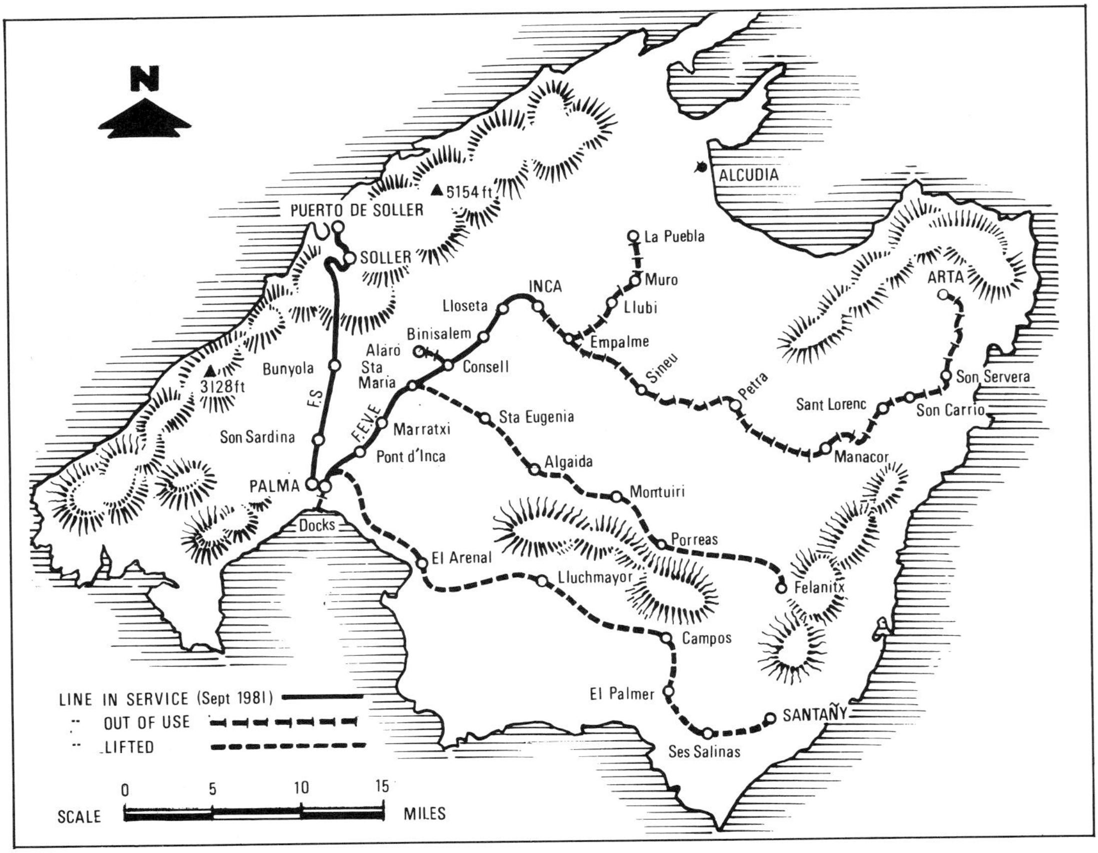

Reminders of the steam age on Majorca;

No 31, a 2-6-0T (Krupp 957/26) on a freight to Palma, at Montuiri in 1960. *M. Swift*

*Below:* By May 1961, the date of this photograph, one of the few steam duties was that of the Palma station pilot. Nasmyth Wilson 4-4-0T No 5 takes water at Palma. *I. Jones*

*Bottom:* The sad remains of 4-4-0T No 24 (built Palma, 1911) and 4-4-0T No 16 (Nasmyth Wilson 526/97) in Palma goods yard, 1960. *M. Swift*

decline which affected traffic for some years, and improvements to the island's roads dealt another blow. As with many other narrow gauge railways, internal combustion was introduced in an effort to cut operating costs, and the first petrol railcar was introduced in 1926. It was soon destroyed by fire, but more examples were purchased in 1930 and these survived. In contrast to the steam passenger stock, the railcars were painted light blue with white upper panels. If traffic was heavy, a four-wheeled coach was added as a trailer, although this dictated running round at the terminus.

A slow decline in the fortunes of the railway system continued until the 1950s. Despite the onset of the package holiday era, the railway was in a bad position to benefit as none of the holiday areas was served, with the exception of the Santany branch which skirted the Bay of Palma and included the towns of C'an Pastilla and El Arenal; these are so near the capital they were vulnerable to road competition.

In 1951, the island railways were nationalised and placed under the control of the Ferrocarriles Economicos de Via Estrecha (FEVE), a loose translation of this grand title being Narrow Gauge Light Railways. FEVE is an association of 22 railways of various gauges throughout Spain, mostly metre gauge , but also including at least one example of the Spanish narrow gauge of 4ft 8½ins. The 5ft 6ins standard gauge lines on the mainland are operated by RENFE. One early result of FEVE control was the reduction of services to two trains daily on each line. Then, from 1956, came an increase in the diesel railcar fleet, with eight more at work by 1960 and a further two in later years. Inevitably, this influx led to the run-down and scrapping of the steam locomotives and carriages, though some of the latter were retained as railcar trailers. The railway network began to contract too. The two-mile branch from Consell to Alaro had already gone in 1935, the neighbouring station being renamed Consell y Alaro. Then, in 1965, came the closure of the line to Santany, followed in 1967 by the last working to Felanitx. Also in 1967, the link between the port of Palma and the rest of the system was closed. This proved to be fatal to the railway goods traffic, as now lorries were more convenient between ship and final delivery without the need for rail transhipment. By 1974, the 132 miles of railway taken over by FEVE had shrunk to 68 miles of route only.

The apparent nadir of the fortunes of the system has been reversed and services have increased. By 1970, there were nine or ten daily departures from Palma, probably made up of four trains each to La Puebla and Arta, with the remainder being short workings terminating at Manacor or Inca. Closures have continued, however. In 1973, trains still served Manacor, and although the line from Inca to Arta has lost its services, the track has not been lifted, unlike those branches closed in the 1960s. In March 1981, the La Puebla branch was closed, buses replacing the trains, although the withdrawal of services may prove to be temporary.

A major change is taking place on the section between Palma and Inca. FEVE is engaged in wholesale reconstruction work to permit higher speeds. The former double track section has been replaced with a single *metre* gauge line. With better ballast, new (straight) sleepers and continuous welded rail, the railway is rapidly losing its traditional narrow gauge image. In September 1981, modern ballast tamping machines contrasted strangely with the rolling, weed-covered track still in use alongside. At that time the station layout at Palma was still under construction. Only one of the original platforms was retained. Departing trains travelled only their own length beyond the end of the station platform before running out of track! To the accompaniment of much horn-blowing by the shunter as he threw over the point levers, echoed by the railcar's whistle, trains then had to set back into a siding beside the departure platform. After another point lever had been thrown to the tune of yet more hooting and whistling, the train would creep off through the engine shed complex to reach the old main line at the station throat. During 1982, a single metre gauge line was in use between Palma and Inca, but eventually two-way working will be restored. The earlier proposal for an extension to Alcudia is being re-examined in the light of tourist development in the north-east of the island, so it is possible that trains may once again run to La Puebla and beyond.

In 1935, the railway owned 38 steam locomotives, four petrol railcars, 85 passenger carriages and 567 goods vehicles. By 1970, this fleet had shrunk to two diesel locomotives, eight railcars, 18 carriages and 81 goods vehicles. From 1980, all but the diesel railcars have been taken out of regular service, though there are now several matching railcar trailers, one with a mail compartment. The remaining four-wheeled goods wagons are all in departmental use, and in any case are mainly hopper wagons on the metre gauge section. A relic of the 3ft days is an old 'birdcage' goods brake van which was sitting on an isolated length of track in Palma goods yard. Quick measurements seemed to indicate that it had metric dimensions and so was not one of the originals.

In complete contrast, Majorca's other railway, the independent Ferrocarril de Soller, is much the same as it was fifty years ago. It was first proposed in 1905, but financial difficulties combined with the problems of tunnelling through the island's northern mountain chain delayed the start of the project. However, construction began in 1907, the tunnel was completed in 1910 and the line opened on 16 April 1912. Although a British-built Falcon 0-4-0 tram locomotive was used for the construction of the line, remaining at work until the 1930s, the rest of the stock was Spanish in origin. The traffic was worked by four 2-6-0Ts built by La Maquinista of Barcelona, the passenger stock comprising ten bogie saloons with tramway-style open balconies. The original fleet of 25 goods wagons was soon increased to 36 vehicles. In 1929, the railway was electrified and its steam engines sold to the Majorca Railways. The FS rolling stock consisted of motor coaches taking power from overhead electrification fed from a sub-station at Bunyola midway along the line; this in turn was supplied from the generating station in Palma. Siemens provided electrical equipment for the motor coaches which were built in Zaragoza.

Leaving the Palma terminus, which is next to the FEVE station, the Soller Railway's single track runs along the centre of the street, partly protected by low hedges. The number of side roads crossing the line mean that the train is whistling almost continuously for right of way at the start of its journey. At one crossing near the terminus a policeman is usually on traffic duty, shaded by a large umbrella set in a socket between the rails. Having stopped the road traffic he has to furl his umbrella as the train approaches! Leaving the town the line skirts a new industrial area before reaching open farmland. There are no fences, but a steady speed is maintained past the first station of Son Sardina, which has a crossing loop, the points being

*Above:* **Palma, December 1975. Railcar No 2006 and trailer No 5003 have just arrived from La Puebla and Inca.** *P. J. Howard*

*Left:* **The station at Binisalem has been spruced up although trains have yet to serve the platform – they were using a dirt platform in 1981. The goods shed is in the background.** *Giles Barnabe*

worked by hand levers fitted with tall indicator discs showing which route is set. After Son Sardina, the gradient slowly steepens as the mountains appear in the distance. The fields gradually give way to pinewoods as the line climbs through the foothills to reach Bunyola, which has the usual loop and also a siding serving a goods shed which is used as a permanent way store. The setting of the station is very attractive and would look almost alpine, but for the dryness of the earth in the surrounding fields. Past Bunyola, climbing starts in earnest through rocky cuttings and over bridges which are little more than girders supporting the rails. As the train passes over them one can look down over the balcony rails and see nothing beneath – a decidedly unsettling experience! The first of an ever-increasing number of short tunnels is threaded as the train ascends towards the summit at 704 ft above Palma, eleven miles distant. The summit itself is attained inside a two-mile tunnel; this is something of an experience when travelling on a forward facing carriage balcony as the tunnel is quite wet in places. Once over the top, the train speeds up noticeably on a deep descent at 1 in 45 for 5¾ miles. Soller is 637 ft below the summit.

Shortly after the long tunnel, tourist trains stop at a station to allow passengers to photograph the peaks surrounding the town of Soller way down on the floor of the valley. On the descent the line runs in and out of the foothills, almost forming a complete spiral curve at one point. Approaching the bottom of the valley houses and lemon groves appear beside the track which for the first time is fenced. The line dives between two large running sheds and the train immediately slows for its arrival at Soller station. This is the operating headquarters of the railway and includes the one-time engine sheds, now used to stable the electric stock. There is also room for storing the trailer coaches, as well as a large goods shed, access to which is by wagon turntable from the central loop in the yard. There are also several end-loading docks in the loading bank, at right-angles to the running lines, an interesting though somewhat inconvenient arrangement. Nowadays, the few freight vehicles seem to be in departmental use only.

Across the station throat from the railway running sheds are the sheds for the narrow gauge trams that complete the journey to Puerto de Soller. This section was too heavily graded for the railway, hence the use of trams. In addition, when the line was built the Palma to Soller section was just too short to qualify for a Government subsidy. By adding another three miles of tramway the Company was able to benefit from the extra money available. The trams are typical examples of early 20th century Continental four-wheelers and usually tow a couple of open-sided toastrack trailers. There is just enough level ground at the top of the hill leading down to the port for the trams to run round their trailers outside the shed.

The FC de Soller's 1929 rolling stock is still in command, complete with varnished body panelling and enormous brass headlamps. During a period when the electrical supply was uncertain, a diesel railcar was bought in 1968. The service comprises five-round trips daily, including a tourist special leaving Palma at 10.40am. This runs non-stop to the photographic station where a short halt is made before completing the journey. The fare is 300 pesetas return for this train (£1.75 at the exchange rate prevailing recently). The normal service return fares are 250 pesetas for first-class, and 215 pesetas for second, but even the tourist fare is good value for two hours of narrow gauge travel through spectacular scenery. The only drawback is that in the season the 10.40am departure attracts crowds rivalling the worst commuter rush-hour, although an unadvertised train runs about 15 minutes ahead

***Below:*** **The new metre gauge tracks and platform at Inca. The 3ft gauge is on the right, with railcars in the siding.** *Giles Barnabe*

***Bottom:*** **Railcar trailer No 5002, with mail compartment. The near end of the vehicle is painted yellow, with red stripes. The rest is painted in the FEVE livery of dark blue and spilt milk with silver stripes.** *Giles Barnabe*

of the tourist special. This returns to Palma soon after reaching Soller, while the tourist special returns after a wait of about 20 minutes at the upper terminus. The return relief is also unadvertised and is lightly used. Indeed, it is possible to have the use of the rear balcony as a private observation car for the return trip – but make sure you have enough film as there is no time to get more at Soller, the station being some way from the town centre.

The latest news of the FS is that the line is due to be upgraded with strengthened bridges. When this work is completed, new rolling stock may be introduced, so the days of varnished woodwork may be numbered.

The visitor may find it difficult to plan trips on the island's railways, not least because the only times given are the departures from the terminus! The writer was in danger of heart failure at Soller having missed what appeared to be the only service returning to Palma in time for the onward connection; in the event the 'extra' train saved the day. Nonetheless, a certain vagueness in operations has always been a feature of the Majorcan railways, and may go some way to explaining the title above the waiting room of the FEVE station in Palma: it simply reads – Sala d'esperanza!

The following have been most helpful in the preparation of this feature: Senor Mathias Mut; P. M. Kalla-Bishop; M. Swift and D. Palmer.

***Above:*** **The Ferrocarril de Soller. Motor coach No 1, built 1929, has just arrived in Palma.**
*Giles Barnabe*

***Left:*** **Motor car No 3 of the Ferrocarril de Soller waits in Soller station, forming the 14.15 to Palma in December 1975.**
*P. J. Howard*

# The Sutton Park Miniature Railway

## D. J. Smith

ONE OF the most attractive miniature railways in Britain was that in Sutton Park, a large area of unspoilt heathland on the outskirts of Birmingham. Near the town gate and within the park boundaries was an area with swings and roundabouts, leased to the Walsall-based showman, Pat Collins. This was redeveloped as winter gardens and an amusement arcade under glass, known as the Crystal Palace. It also became the site for W.J. Bassett-Lowke's third miniature railway in Britain.

Two years earlier, W.J. Bassett-Lowke, the Northampton modelmaker, had founded a subsidiary company known as Miniature Railways of Great Britain, to exploit a boom in passenger-carrying lines of small scale and gauge. The original intention of MR of GB was to provide finished items, spares and construction teams for other owners, but W.J. Bassett-Lowke further decided to become an operator on his own account, leasing sites in different parts of the country, mainly at holiday resorts.

The first line to be operated by the new concern was an experimental 10½in gauge layout (out and back) on waste ground near the entrance of Abington Park, Northampton. It ran throughout the Easter holiday period of 1905. Its single locomotive, an 0-4-4T then known as *The Nipper,* headed a train of three four-wheeled coaches. The experiment proved a great success and served as a curtain-raiser for a larger and more elaborate 15in gauge railway on the South Shore Pleasure Beach at Blackpool. This opened six weeks later in 1905.

Unused equipment from Abington Park was relaid in Sutton Park, next to the Crystal Palace, on ground sub-leased from Pat Collins. The railway opened during the summer of 1907 and was worked by *The Nipper,* later renamed *Rover.* It was a straight and single line about 400 yards in length, the main engineering feature being a single-span bridge with side parapets over a shallow stream. The line ran in the direction of Windley Pool, a boating pool near Windley Gate, partly hidden by woodland bordering the park. After a short period it was decided to increase the gauge from 10½in to 15in, for improved safety and increased traffic. This entailed a renewal of stock, *Rover* giving place to an Atlantic-type *Mighty Atom,* a sister engine of the famed *Little Giant* then working at Blackpool. Trains usually comprised four open 12-seater coaches with toastrack seating. The running track was extended even nearer to Windley Pool, with a return loop at the far end guarded by self-operating points. The second version of the line was opened in 1908, operating in much the same form until World War 1. During the early years, there was one serious accident when a small boy was crushed to death on the single-span bridge, wedged between a moving train and the parapet.

In 1909, there was a further change of motive power as *Mighty Atom* was borrowed by W.J. Bassett-Lowke to run at a prestigious engineering exhibition at Nancy, France. *Mighty Atom* was shipped abroad at short notice, to be replaced by a Cagney (American) 4-4-0 locomotive, on loan from

***Below:*** **Sutton Coldfield, 1910.** ***Mighty Atom*** **and train.** *J. G. Tidmarsh Collection*

***Above left:*** **SMR, Easter Monday 1958. No 1 *Sutton Belle* arrives on a three-coach train. No 2 *Sutton Flyer* is waiting to couple on to the rear of the set.**
*J. G. Tidmarsh*

***Above:*** **SMR terminal station, c. 1948. *Prince of Wales* heads the train.** *J. Wilkins*

an estate railway at Blakesley Hall near Towcester; the owner was a friend and client of W.J. Bassett-Lowke. The Cagney engine was certainly no beauty and far from being a scale model, but as a reliable 'workhorse' remained until World War 1, during which passenger services were suspended. During the war much of the park was used for military training with a reception camp for newly enlisted recuits. It is thought that part of the line was lifted and used as a contractor's railway, during the construction of a hutted camp.

Shortly before the outbreak of World War 1, Miniature Railways of Great Britain had been absorbed into a larger organisation, also controlled by Bassett-Lowke, known as Narrow Gauge Railways Limited. The company was active at Rhyl, Fairbourne (near Barmouth) and Ravenglass. It seemed to lose interest in what was then known as The Crystal Palace Railway, which by mutual consent was relinquished to Pat Collins, but in a greatly rundown condition. From 1923, the railway remained unworked and eventually overgrown for the next fourteen years. Pat Collins may well have been tempted to cut his losses and abandon the project, but for the interest and enthusiasm of his wife. She seems to have formed a sentimental attachment for the 'toy trains', always hoping that the line might be restored. *Mighty Atom* had been sold to a miniature railway in Southport, but was resold in 1930 to a family named Parkinson who operated a narrow gauge system at Great Yarmouth.

In 1937, it was decided to reopen the line in Sutton Park. By a strange coincidence, the Parkinsons were eager to sell out at Great Yarmouth and so Pat Collins bought their line and equipment as it stood. It was understood that the Parkinsons should use their expertise to rebuild and enlarge the Sutton line, a task that was completed twelve months later. The third layout, almost a mile in length, included an extensive balloon loop near Windley Pool, with a combined station and engine shed at the Crystal Palace end. There was also an engine spur and turntable in the station area, but these were little-used after the first few weeks. Track within the station included an engine release loop for running round the train. Falling gradients on the layout were 1 in 60 with rising gradients of 1 in 80, favouring what eventually became the outward or clockwise circuit.

The motive power of the renewed line was an electric outline locomotive, powered by a 10 hp internal combustion engine as well as *Prince of Wales*, the former *Mighty Atom*. *Prince of Wales* had been considerably altered at Southport and

***Above:* Official postcard of the line, showing No 1 *Sutton Belle* and train in their ultimate livery, 1957.** *W. T. Hunt*

Great Yarmouth, having acquired smoke deflectors, new splashers and outside bearings for the trailing bogie. New rolling stock included a rake of totally enclosed passenger coaches, designed and made by the Parkinsons, turned out in attractive maroon livery.

The Sutton line was kept running throughout World War 2, helping to provide recreation for those encouraged to spend their holidays at home. Yet conditions on the layout were often far from ideal, what with the shortage of spares and low standards of maintenance. Both locomotives began to show signs of wear, the whole line taking on a shabby appearance, especially after 1942. At one time a tall stovepipe was added to the chimney of *Prince of Wales* to facilitate steaming, but it looked odd and strangely out of scale.

In 1946, the line was sold to Mr T.G. Hunt of Oldbury, head of a Black Country engineering firm and a miniature railway enthusiast. The official title of the Crystal Palace Railway was now dropped in favour of Sutton Miniature Railway, the initials SMR being painted on all items of rolling stock and motive power. Mr Hunt also acquired two little-used Atlantic locomotives from a former garden railway near Tewkesbury, and a rake of open coaches. The locomotives were named *Sutton Belle* and *Sutton Flyer* respectively, being modifications of the Bassett-Lowke Class 30 or improved 'Little Giant' class. *Sutton Belle* appeared in a crimson livery, but *Sutton Flyer* was even more attractive in a shade of Great Eastern blue that seemed ideal for a small-scale locomotive. A miniature railcar was eventually acquired from the 15in gauge system at Dudley Zoo. It was operated on wet days – between showers – as, unlike steam locomotives, it could be prepared at short notice. The railcar had a 20 hp Morris Commercial engine, and its outline was based on the first Great Western Railway streamlined railcar of 1934. It usually drew a short, mixed train of closed and open stock.

The popularity of the Sutton line seemed to increase with the years, especially during the period of the International Scout Jamboree, held in Sutton Park during the summer of 1957. On the average Bank Holiday the railway was expected to cope with at least 8,000 passengers, the postwar record for one day being 12,000. The future seemed assured, yet in 1962 the railway closed at the end of the summer season. This was because the lease of the Crystal Palace site expired on 7 October 1962, affecting the miniature railway as this was covered by the same legal rules and stipulations as the winter gardens. The freehold of the site had reverted to Sutton Council and it was the policy of the park owners to preserve only its natural beauties, banning all mechanical amusements, slot machines and side-shows. The railway, nothing if not mechanical, had to go. Nothing was left of the layout apart from the contours of cuttings and embankments and these were rapidly choked by weeds and undergrowth. Considering that the railway fitted into a small area on the borders of the park enhancing rather than spoiling its surroundings, the decision not to maintain the amenity seems somehow short-sighted and was taken without reference to local feeling.

# Back to front locomotives

## D. R. Carling

A NUMBER of classes of steam locomotives were designed to run normally in what appeared to be the backward direction, as distinct from tank engines that ran either way more or less indiscriminately. A few tank engines were intended to be driven normally cab-first, such as the 0-6-2T locomotives built by Beyer, Peacock & Co. in 1888 for the La Guaira & Caracas Railway or the 2-4-2T for the Ferries and Cliff House Railroad of San Francisco, built by Baldwin in 1887, but, except for the cab front and the position of the headlight and cowcatcher, they were structurally normal. We shall be concerned with tender engines with the whole, or a large part of the normal structure reversed.

The great majority of such locomotives were North American and all but one belonged to one railway. However, there were also some successful examples in Europe – as well as one experiment that didn't quite come off – and one European-built class in South America.

At the Paris Exhibition of 1900, a number of locomotives were on display. One that attracted particular attention was a six-coupled bogie express passenger engine (effectively an – 0-6-4) built to the design of Signor Planchar at the Florence works of the Rete Adriatica (Adriatic System) of the Italian Southern Railway (Strade Ferrate Meridionali). The pecularity of this locomotive was that all the coupled wheels were under the boiler barrel and the bogie was under the firebox and cab, which latter was fully enclosed. Fuel was carried in two bunkers looking like short side tanks while the water was contained in a cylindrical three-axle tank wagon, complete with a brakesman's cabin at one end. This vehicle was coupled, either way round, to the chimney end of the locomotive.

This locomotive, No 3701, proved so successful in service, with an unusually low coal consumption, that 16 more, with detail variations, were ordered in 1902, some from Borsig in Berlin and some from Breda in Milan. They were followed by 14 more from Breda in 1905/06, for the newly formed Italian State Railway (F S). Twelve more were delivered in 1913.

On test, No 3701, the original locomotive, attained 78-79mph being designed for 110km/h (68.75mph) although the line limit was then only 90 (56mph). These – 0-6-4s were four-cylinder compounds on the Italian system, with one inside and one outside high-pressure cylinder on one side and an inside and an outside low-pressure cylinder on the other. This asymmetrical arrangement had several advantages. It ensured very good balancing and the use of only two sets of valve gear, with one valve for the two high-pressure cylinders, and one for the two low-pressure cylinders as the inside and outside cranks on each side were effectively at 180° to one another, but still providing different, but related, cut-offs in the high- and low-pressure cylinders, respectively. This gave a more even division of work between high- and low-pressure cylinders and better efficiency. An adequate receiver volume could also be provided. The

***Below:*** **Italian State Railways -0-6-4 of Class 670 (fourth series).**

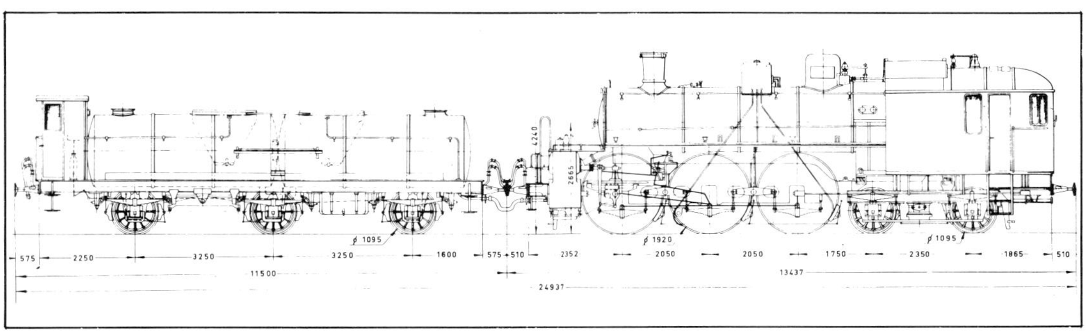

locomotives acquired the sobriquet 'Mucca', the Italian for 'Cow'.

One of the Italian locomotives was used for early experiments with the Franco-Crosti system of feed-water heating. The tender was altered to carry the pre-heater, the products of combustion passing through an articulated pipe from the smokebox, being ejected through a chimney near the back of the tender. The exhaust steam was also conveyed to be exhaused through this chimney. One of the 'Muccas' was used as a counter-pressure brake locomotive for controlled testing of other locomotives, later receiving the Riggenbach counter-pressure brake. Some of the 'Muccas' were later superheated.

From 1907 onwards, the Italian State Railways had a numerous class of 0-10-0 locomotives similarly arranged as regards the coal bunker and the water tender, which could be coupled at either end of the engine. The 0-10-0s were structurally normal and probably more often ran forwards than backwards, and so do not come within the scope of this survey.

The correct description of the wheel arrangement of the 'Muccas' is a matter of interest. As a vehicle, they were 4-6-0s, but structurally and mechanically they were 0-6-4s. To resolve the difficulty it seems reasonable to put a minus sign in front of the notation, making it − 0-6-4. This designation is even more to the point for most of the American locomotives where the structure was more complex.

The next European reversed engine was one of the three high-speed streamlined 4-6-4s of Class '05' of the Deutsche Reichsbahn Geselschaft. Two of them, delivered by Borsig early in 1935, were normally arranged hand-fired engines, using mainly lump coal of high quality.

In 1933, Henschel & Sohn of Kassel had put forward a project for a reversed 4-6-4, with oil-firing. Oil was expensive and relatively in short supply in Germany so the authorities decided to attempt the much more difficult task of using pulverised coal. The main object was to provide a better outlook for the crew, clearly important when high speeds were being sustained over long distances. Unfortunately, the first two locomotives left something to be desired.

The third prototype was delivered in 1937, over eighteen months behind schedule. Great difficulty had been found in getting the pneumatic coal conveyor to work properly. The locomotive was never really satisfactory because at differing rates of firing the coaldust was apt to become unevenly distributed, or cause partial blockage. At best, the output of the locomotive was appreciably limited. This may have been due both to the quality of the available coal and to the inevitable bends in the pipeline. Eventually, it was decided to rebuild the locomotive for normal hand firing in 1944, the engine being 'turned round' for chimney-first operation. This third prototype differed in what became the trailing bogie, this having inside instead of outside frames. All three locomotives had their streamlined casings removed in time.

***Top:*** **The Beyer, Peacock 0-6-2+0-6-2 Meyer, with tender, built for Bolivia in 1911.** *North Western Museum of Science and Industry*

***Above:*** **Cutaway diagram of Henschel proposed reversed 4-6-4, dated 1933.**

***Right:*** **The third Henschel reversed 4-6-4, No 05.003, built 1937.** *LPC/Ian Allan Library*

The South American locomotives were of a very rare breed – Meyers with separate tenders. The Meyer was usually a tank engine. There seem to have been only two classes of such locomotives. Kitson's built an 0-6-0+0-6-0 Kitson-Meyer for the Cape Government Railways in 1903, two more for the Rhodesia Railways in the same year and one in 1904 for the Central South African Railway. Each lot featured some variation of dimensions, but all engines usually worked chimney-first with the water tender coupled behind the coal bunker. The other class of six was built by Beyer, Peacock in 1913 and was of the 0-6-2+0-6-2 type; in this case, the tender

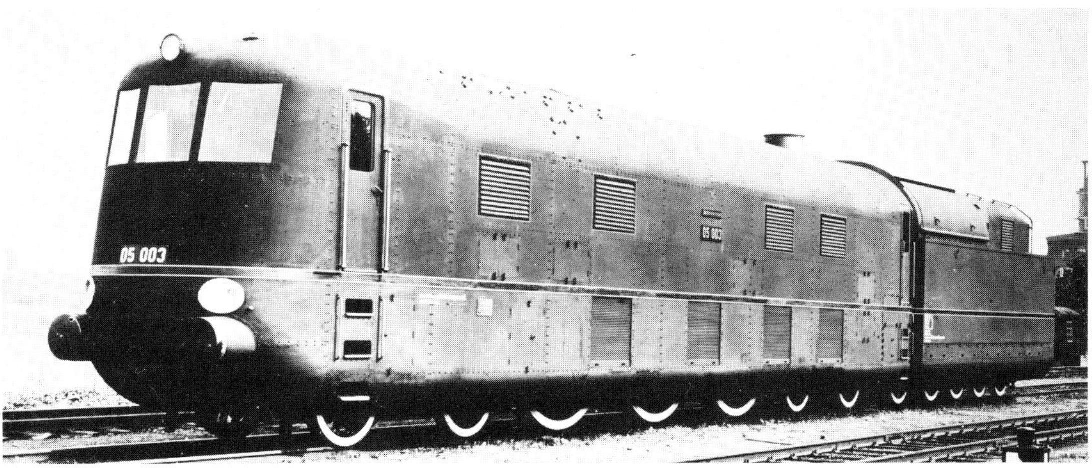


was coupled at the chimney end. There has been much confusion about these locomotives, which were known as Livesey-Meyers and were built for the Bolivia Railway to the order of the Antofagasta (Chili) & Bolivia Railway.

The Bolivia Railway was always of metre gauge, but the Antofagasta, who operated it, was originally 2ft 6in gauge. Consequently, both track gauges have been quoted for these engines and differing figures given for various other dimensions. The main line of the Bolivia Railway lies between 12,000 and 13,000ft above sea level and branches rise to 13,500 and 15,800ft, with the result that the cabs were totally enclosed for protection against the cold. The locomotives were normally driven with the coal bunker leading so that each bogie ran like a normal 2-6-0. The original tenders were rectangular tanks with a rack on top. This held a reserve of four tons of coal carried in bags, and supplemented the main supply on the engine itself. Later, plain cylindrical cistern wagons were used.

Turning now to North America, the first locomotive to be noted was originally a normal wood-burning 'American' 4-4-0 built by Baldwin for the North Pacific Coast Railroad, a 3ft gauge line in northern California involved with the haulage of timber and forest products. In 1900, this 4-4-0 was rebuilt with a special oil-fired water-tube boiler with a cylindrical firebox, and it was one of the first few in the United States to use oil fuel. The frame, cylinders, wheels and machinery remained as usual, only the boiler and cab being reversed. The latter was closed in to suit the now normal cab-first running. At the chimney end, the tender consisted of a flat car with two upright cylindrical tanks, one each for water and fuel. The locomotive ran in this form until 1910.

All the remaining locomotives to be dealt with were in service on the Southern Pacific Railroad. All were articulated and all were built by Baldwin. The earlier examples were Mallet compounds, but the majority were simple expansion. All the compounds were eventually converted to single expansion, two of them having tender boosters added.

The Southern Pacific's first Mallets were two normal 2-8-8-2 compounds, with the high pressure cylinders on the rear unit and the low on the articulated front unit. Built in 1909, they were claimed then to be the largest locomotives on any railroad. They were also oil-burners, as were all the others to be described. When these 2-8-8-2s were put into service on the old Central Pacific main line, with its numerous tunnels and very long snowsheds, so much steam and hot gas came back into the cab that the crews were almost asphyxiated, besides finding the heat intolerable. Otherwise, the locomotives proved very satisfactory.

To overcome the difficulties experienced by the crews of the 2-8-8-2s and also to improve forward vision over a route with many sharp curves, it was decided that the next batch of locomotives should be built with the cab at the leading end. The whole engine was reversed, boiler, frames, cylinders and all, and the tender coupled at the chimney end. This was easily done on an oil-burner.

There were 15 locomotives in this batch, built 1909/10, and the two original ones were modified to the back to front arrangement. Additional orders followed and by 1913 there were 49 of these heavy

***Above:*** **Southern Pacific compound-2-6-6-4 No 4208, built Baldwin 1911, and rebuilt in reversed form by SP in 1921.**

***Below:*** **Southern Pacific-2-8-8-4 No 4133, built Baldwin 1930.** *LPC/Ian Allan Library*

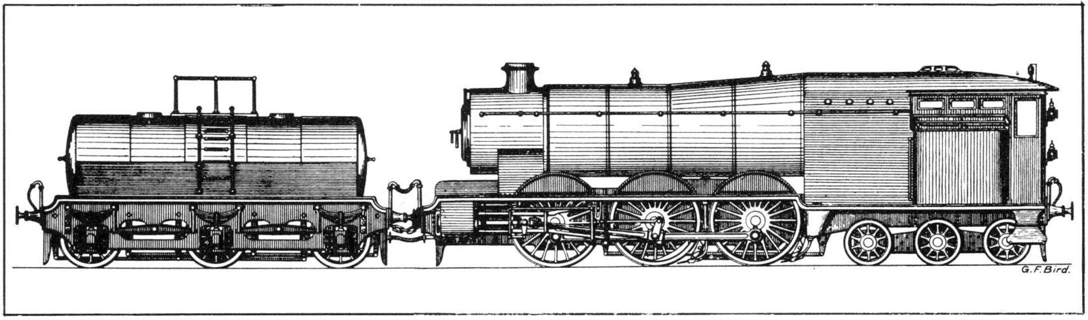


*Above:* **The remarkable uncredited essay for an -0-6-6, described in *The Locomotive Magazine* of 15 August 1903.** *Ian Allan Library*

freight engines in service, as well as 12 2-6-6-2 passenger engines built in 1911.

Experience with the passenger engines soon caused the leading two-wheeled truck to be replaced by a four-wheeled bogie, to produce a safer and smoother running vehicle and also reducing flange wear. These locomotives have been classified as 4-6-6-2s, but this is misleading as they were structurally 2-6-6-4s in all respects, except that the four-wheeled truck was a normal leading type bogie with a central pivot. It could not be compared with the later type of four-wheeled Delta truck at the trailing end, which had its pivot at the front. Moreover, the normal arrangement of articulation was retained with the boiler fixed to the main frame and the unit at the chimney end pivoted. The high- and low-pressure cylinders were arranged as usual on a Mallet.

It seems reasonable to call these locomotives – 2-6-6-4s. Even the 2-8-8-2 and 2-6-6-2 types are not properly described without the minus sign, given that they had the pivoted unit at the chimney, or trailing, end and the cylinders at the rear of each unit.

By 1928, these compounds were regarded as too slow for the operating requirements and so one of the – 2-8-8-2s was rebuilt as a four-cylinder simple. The conversion was successful and, by mid-1929, seven more had been converted, as well as two – 2-6-6-4s. Not only that, but ten new and larger – 2-8-8-4s were put into service in the autumn of 1928, and these were simples from the start. These engines performed so well that 16 more were ordered in March 1929 and delivered in the same year.

In 1930, 25 – 2-8-8-4s of an improved type were added to the Southern Pacific's locomotive roster. The boiler pressure was raised from 235 to 250 lb/sq in and there were various detailed improvements. It was mid-1936 when 12 more – 2-8-8-4s were ordered, and 14 more followed that December. The main differences from the 1930 batch involved the use of cast-steel engine beds for each unit, including cylinders, valve chests etc, and disc-type driving and coupled wheels. The tenders were considerably larger than before.

Twenty-eight similar locomotives were built in 1939, and no less than 70 in 1942, in two batches of 40 and 30. Another 10 were delivered in each of the years 1943 and 1944. By then, 195 had been constructed of these – 2-8-8-4 back-to-front locomotives, besides the dozen – 2-6-6-4s rebuilt from – 2-8-8-2s, and the 49 – 2-8-8-2s. All but three of the – 2-8-8-2s and all the – 2-6-6-4s were still running when the last – 2-8-8-4 was delivered. At that stage, the Southern Pacific had a maximum of 253 cab-first engines in service simultaneously.

With 43 'Muccas', two single specimens, six Livesey-Meyers and 256 Southern Pacific cab-in-front engines this makes a grand total of 307 reversed locomotives.

Mention may also be made of an unrealised proposal for a – 0-6-6 similar to a 'Mucca', but apparently intended for the British loading gauge. This design appeared in the *Locomotive Magazine* in 1903 and, though the article is anonymous, the author is of the opinion that it was most probably due to A.M. Bell.

This locomotive was to have been a four-cylinder compound with high-pressure cylinders outside and low inside. It seemed to be a mixture of Planchar's general arrangement, a Churchward-style taper boiler (but with a wide firebox), and French, possibly de Glehn, compounding. It was innocent of superheating, and the inside connecting rods based on those used for the Great Eastern 'Decapod'. The coal bunkers were placed alongside the cab. The square grate had an area of 37.5 sq ft and the total heating surface was 2,402 sq ft, with boiler pressure 200 lb/sq in, or more. The 6ft diameter coupled wheels were shaped on a rigid wheelbase of 13ft 0in and the engine wheelbase was 29ft 3in. The bunker capacity was only two tons, unless two tons each side were intended.

The cylinders were to be 15 and 23½in in diameter by 24in stroke. It would be interesting to know for what kind of duty on express trains the locomotive was intended and for which railway.

# Viewpoints

Some different perspectives on the British railway scene.

***Right:*** **Even the mundane can be made interesting . . . the interior of a Class 405 (4-SUB) electric multiple unit.** *J. G. Glover*

***Below:*** **But where is level ground? The tree to the right gives some clue in this study of the flying junctions outside Greenford station, in July 1981. The Greenford–West Ealing line dips beneath the LT Central Line. A West Ruislip-bound Central Line train approaches.** *Brian Morrison*

***Far right:*** **A dramatic railwayscape, seen near Irvine in 1982. The train consists of two Class 126 diesel multiple-units forming a Glasgow–Ayr working, and in their last weeks of active service.** *Ian Betteley*

***Below right:*** **At first sight, this might be a 1950s' view of a 'Castle' heading out of Birmingham for Paddington. But the present-day cityscape destroys the illusion fostered by the Victorian viaduct. 'Castle' No 5051 heads the 'Devonian' charter train away from Birmingham Moor St station on 9 October 1982.** *David Olsen Hopper*

Z45

# A day with Córas Iompair Éireann

## David St John Thomas

IRISH railways are very Irish, a greater contrast from British Rail than are the railways of most of the rest of the English-speaking world. That is the feeling I always return with after renewing an emotional acquaintance with Córas Iompair Éireann (CIE).

Not long ago, I had to pay an unexpected short visit for evening events in Dublin on Sunday and Cork on Monday. Having Monday afternoon and evening free, I decided to take the train to Waterford via Kilkenny (a route new to me) and then (since there is no afternoon train from Waterford to Limerick Junction) to go by hire car. British Airways duly confirmed that Avis had a car available and that I could drop it off at Cork airport on my way home on Tuesday.

So at 7 am on Monday morning I left one of Dublin's northern suburbs soon to be served by electrified railway. I had to go by taxi since there is no convenient link to Heuston station, an imposing stone block of a building inconveniently far from the centre. Once it looked as though Heston would be closed and trains from the south be rerouted via the outskirts to Connolly. Instead Heuston has gained two platforms, making five. The new ones, two sides of an island, have been fitted into the middle of the station where carriage sidings once stood. They make the station far more flexible, and prevent the delays that occurred over many years to up trains; extra services or late running often resulted in trains being halted at every appropriate signal many miles back out into the country.

Traditionally, rather less than a score of daily trains have arrived at Heuston, which has no suburban traffic, but they have always tended to be bunched, with periods of hectic activity after long lulls. This is still partially true, though among the 21 winter Tuesday-Saturday arrivals (two extras on Mondays) there is now a more evenly spaced service from Cork.

This was my first visit to Heuston since the new platforms had been opened and I was pleased to see that they had been given the chequered black-and-white tile treatment that is a feature of all major CIE stations. It was also the first time I had seen BR Mark 2 air-conditioned stock in CIE's black and tan

***Left:*** **Platform indicators, Dublin Heuston.** *CIE*

***Above right:*** **The 15.10 Waterford–Dublin Heuston at Muine Bheag on 23 June 1980, headed by General Motors 2,450 hp Co-Co No 083.** *P. A. Brown*

***Right:*** **Lucan South, on the Dublin–Cork line. '071' class Co-Co No 074 on the 18.00 Dublin Heuston–Westport, 15 July 1978.** *Wm S. Watson*

083
CIE

CIE

livery bringing greater luxury though, of course, not making use of the wider loading gauge. A ten-coach set formed the 07.30 departure for Cork, the day's first train out of Heuston.

My 07.40 to Waterford, six coaches including the heating van, left from one of the new platforms with around 100 passengers but minus the advertised buffet car; a story all too familiar in Britain – the steward had not turned up. Twenty minutes on our way we passed the day's first up train, one of the Monday-only extras, from Waterford.

Heuston used largely to be involved in handling Irish people going to Britain and overseas visitors bound for southern Ireland via Dun Laoghaire, transferring from the ship into a special train run around Dublin to Heuston. The train no longer runs, having been withdrawn as part of electrification work and anyway traffic has declined: fewer visitors come to Ireland and more of those who do fly or bring their cars. Today, therefore, Heuston is more concerned with taking the Irish about their own business, and weekend traffic in particular has boomed. Fourteen trains now depart on Sundays in place of the single one of the immediate postwar era. And Friday evening and Monday morning traffic is also very heavy.

At our first stop, Droichead Nua, we were joined by a handful of passengers, but about 70 were on the up platform as an extremely full 05.00 from Cork arrived. At Kildare we stopped beside the next up service, a Mondays-only train from Galway.

And so on to track new to me, the single line of the Waterford branch, crossing another packed up train at Carlow, with a sniff of the bacon and eggs being served in the day's only full restaurant car on the route. At Kilkenny, following rationalisation of routes to Waterford, you reverse; one of the much-publicised Dublin-Waterford liner trains was in the freight yard.

As in most of inland Ireland, the scenery was pleasant, undulating without being dramatic, few signs of habitation away from the occasional village, but the inevitable ruin to remind of troubled days. The speed of CIE trains between stations on single lines is surprisingly high, but approaches to stations are always taken cautiously.

At Waterford, the Limerick line and then the rusting track of the long-closed Mallow route joined us as we slowly approached the station, already busy with people waiting for the return 10.55 to Dublin. After a short look round, I crossed the river and began enquiring as to which garage had the Avis agency. None was the answer! British Airways had boobed. Worse than that, no other car hire firm had a vehicle free, and a travel agent said there were no buses or planes. I could hitch, or wait for the 20.35 which would get me to Cork at 00.30 next morning (too late, of course, for my appointment) or had I thought about it earlier I could return by the 10.55.

But it was now 10.50 and I'd never walk back in time. A request to be driven was at first refused but then accepted. Running through red lights, we just made it, in time indeed to buy a ticket.

At first I bemoaned the fact that I had only bought a Dublin-Waterford single at £12.50; a day return would have cost the same. But though I had to change at Droichead Nua, the very first station out of Dublin, and go roughly three times the mileage of the direct route, I was charged by the latter, £10. Yes, I went a lot of miles for that £10!

The train was very full, the five-across seating in the open stock being put to good use. No catering service was even supposed to be provided, and by now feeling extremely hungry I dashed down the hill to buy biscuits while the locomotive was running round the train at the Kilkenny reversal. And so back to the main line at Kildare. We were late and I thought we might delay the seasonal Mondays, Fridays and Saturdays 10.30 from Dublin to Tralee, first stop Rathluirc (between Limerick Junction and Mallow); but it passed us at speed near the Curragh racecourse.

At Droichead Nua, over the bridge to join the 12.55 from Dublin to Cork. 'I remember you,' said an employee. 'You used to be booking clerk here years ago.' I told him it was my first time ever at Droichead Nua. 'What a coincidence,' he said. 'You are just as tall as the man I remember.' It recalled the time when, sitting beside the driver of a County Donegal Railways train, I admitted that indeed I came from England. 'That is a great coincidence; my daddy was once there.'

It was now that the real Irishness of the traffic could be studied. Though no train had called since that on which I had travelled to Waterford,

***Above:* Contrast in styles at Limerick Junction, June 1978. Ex-GSWR '101' 0-6-0 No 186, in the care of the Railway Preservation of Ireland and carrying a fictitious livery for filming purposes, was working a main line rail tour. '001' class Co-Co No 052 passed on a southbound block freight train.** *D. Trevor Rowe*

numerous passengers arrived and discussed their travel plans with the patient booking clerk. Pricing is even more complex than on BR, with concessions according to how many main line rail journeys you make annually and the size of your family, as well as which trains you travel by and when you return.

'But supposing one of them should feel homesick, can they come back earlier?' Priests and nuns seemed the best informed on what the deal was. The employee who thought I was a former colleague confirmed that occasional freight (containers only) was still handled at the station – and shephered us all (about 40, including five who had changed from the Waterford train) to the very rear of the platform; 'even if you're going Super Standard class, they won't let you straight into it, and the restaurant car that comes next will be locked.'

Of course I made straight for the restaurant car, with happy memories of CIE catering on former occasions. Meat dishes cost up to nearly £10, but egg, bacon and sausage automatically accompanied by a stock of brown and white bread, pats of butter, jam and tea or coffee, was a reasonable £4.45. No table setting, each person given his own tray. Business was brisk. But then, again, the train was full.

At Kildare, which we should have run through non-stop, we crossed first to the up track and then into the up platform loop, crowded with passengers. There beside us on the down main line was the 12.15 to Tralee, which nearly an hour before we had passed at speed only a mile or so away.

Rathluirc, Mallow and Cork passengers – the last should have changed at Mallow – were transferring to us, though even if we regained our own lost time, they would still arrive an hour late.

'People are standing,' came the report from the stream of customers for lunch and for drinks at the bar. So, the £10 Waterford-Cork fare seeming a real bargain, I decided to splurge on a £5 supplement to get into Super Standard class, still labelled first-class, though first-class as such has long been abolished in Ireland. Most trains have only Standard class accommodation, but prestige expresses have a single Super Standard class coach, just like a BR open first, at the end furthest from Dublin, next to the restaurant car. You can indeed be served food and drink at your own seat, and as an afterthought I had dessert there.

Though the train as a whole was crowded, there were only a dozen of us in this little club. Predictably, several were priests, always among the keenest supporters of first-class in the old days, and overseas visitors, notably Californian university students. Distinctly not the talkative cross-section of ordinary Irish people I had travelled with to and from Waterford.

Last time I went down the main line to Cork was on the locomotive, single-manned by the father of 16 children. I remember well, since his repeatedly telling me how poor he was and how rich I must be was mistaken by me as a hint he should be tipped. When I proferred a note at the end of the journey he made a pretty speech: 'I've no doubt I need it, and

*Above:* **A set of CIE's AC stock, built at Derby by British Rail Engineering Ltd, forms the 18.10 'Supertrain' from Dublin Heuston–Waterford, passing Lucan South on 15 July 1978 behind the GM '071' class-leader.** *Wm S. Watson*

I've no doubt you can afford it – or more. But you've helped me bring the train into Cork on time as a good colleague and colleagues don't tip each other.' Since those days a considerable amount of continuously welded rail has been put in, but I thought the general standard of maintenance had deteriorated, resulting in slower overall speeds, though most trains now make more stops, and this has encouraged traffic at the ten intermediate stations now open. Indeed, throughout Ireland, it is unusual for a train to stop without substantial business being transacted. There is now only one Sunday Cork-Dublin non-stop.

Our busiest intermediate stop was of course Limerick Junction, where nearly 100 passengers alighted. Alas, most of them were going to be further delayed, the branch train for Limerick having left five minutes before so as to be able to maintain a connection from Limerick into the up afternoon mail. Though these days main line trains do not have to back into the station, Limerick Junction remains an interesting, uniquely Irish place. I recall L. T. C. Rolt's colourful description of it with two steam locomotives facing each other only a few yards apart at the only time in the whole week that there was activity in a wartime Ireland starved of coal. Limerick business is good, but except for the up morning and down evening businessmen's train which takes the loop avoiding the Junction, all services involve a change. Except on Sundays, the Nenagh line is run as a self-contained branch for the benefit of intermediate station traffic only.

At Rathluirc over 30 passengers alighted, and at Mallow more than I could sensibly count. Those for Kilarney and Tralee were told to remain on the same platform and catch the next train; the 10.55 from Dublin was obviously behind us, well over an hour late, but was to precede the 15.40 Cork-Tralee which arrived at the next platform during our stay. Further delays must have occurred as the two trains running block to block down the branch had to cross the evening Tralee-Cork train.

I had now spent nine hours on CIE, most of them on the main line, and had not seen a single freight train on the move. But between Mallow and Cork we passed a container and a tanker train, and as I left Cork station and walked across the road bridge immediately in front of the tunnel-mouth, a second train of tankers came around the goods loop, its locomotive roaring as speed was gathered for the steep climb up through the tunnel. No station could be harder for main line trains to start from than Cork, but I never tire of the station itself with its spacious concourse complete with steam locomotive on display and the suburban platforms for the Cobh line.

It was an enforced day on CIE, but one I shall always remember.

# Cheltenham perspective

## E. C. B. Thornton

FROM THE opening in 1908 of the GWR Birmingham – Stratford upon Avon – Cheltenham route and for some years after, there were two GWR expresses over the line, the morning northbound one named 'The Shakespeare Express' and one southbound then un-named, but locally known as 'The West of England Express'. Many years after, this became officially 'The Cornishman'. In the late afternoon, the return services in the opposite direction came through. The 'Shakespeare Express' originally ran via Leamington Spa, Rugby LNWR and Peterborough to Norwich, but a year after opening of the new line was diverted to Birmingham Snow Hill and Birkenhead. Its coaches then carried roof-boards bearing the words 'Shakespeare Express Birkenhead, Chester, Stratford-on-Avon and Bristol'. The West of England Express bore the words 'Wolverhampton, Birmingham, Plymouth and Penzance via Stratford on Avon'. As Cheltonians we were very proud of these trains.

Their route south and west of Cheltenham Lansdown Junction was over the virtually joint line with the Midland (the GWR and the MR owned half the distance each) to Engine Shed Junction, Gloucester, then over the Gloucester avoiding line to Gloucester South Junction, and the former South Wales main line as far as Standish Junction. There they crossed over on to the parallel Midland line on which they continued by operation of running powers as far as Yate. At the Bristol end of this station they diverged to the left, the northbound line flying over the Midland lines, to Westerleigh North Junction, the apex of a triangle, to Westerleigh West Junction where the South Wales direct line was joined and used as far as Stoke Gifford. There they diverged again via Stapleton Road to Bristol Temple Meads. In fact, this is the route of present-day trains from Birmingham which do not call at Gloucester. With at least five severe and two lesser speed restrictions between Cheltenham and Bristol for junctions, the route was not a high-speed one and the distance between Birmingham and Bristol was 11 miles longer than that of the Midland's from New Street.

Until about 1923, the engines working these GWR expresses were 4-4-0s. The 'Shakespeare Express' and two other trains had 'Cities' or 'Flowers', but the West of England express had a 'County' 4-4-0. Occasionally, the de Glehn Compound 4-4-2 *La France* was used. It was not

***Below:*** **Midland & South Western Junction Railway 4-4-2T No 18 on a local train at Cheltenham Lansdown station in pre-Grouping days.**
*Ian Allan Library*

until after World War 1 when the GWR increased its stud of 'Star' 4-6-0s with the 'Abbeys' series and embarked on the 'Castles' that the 'County' 4-4-0s were displaced by 'Saint' 4-6-0s. But the snag was that the Midland/LMS imposed a 30 mph speed restriction on Stonehouse viaduct for 4-6-0 engines only – a dirty trick because the MR had no 4-6-0s and so was not affected! I believe that some years later, when the LMS started using Class '5' or 'Jubilee' 4-6-0s, it strengthened the viaduct and removed the restriction. By then, the GWR trains were in the hands of 'Stars' and 'Castles'. A number of coal and goods trains from South Wales ran via Gloucester, Cheltenham and the Honeybourne line and were hauled by '28xx' 2-8-0s with 4ft 7½in driving wheels.

Before World War 2, the first diesel buffet railcar in England ran between South Wales and Birmingham Snow Hill and return daily via the Honeybourne line.

One curious train over the Honeybourne which ran for many years was the 4.45pm from Paddington. This slipped a coach at Moreton-in-Marsh which was then worked forward to Honeybourne where it reversed and went on to Cheltenham Malvern Road. There it again reversed and finished up at St James' terminus shortly before 8.0pm. This working filled an otherwise awkward gap in the London to Cheltenham service between the 3.15pm and 6.15 trains via Swindon, but was effectively killed as a London to Cheltenham train by the introduction of the 'Cheltenham Spa Express' at 5.0pm from Paddington via Swindon.

The local train service between Cheltenham and Honeybourne was operated by the delightful GWR steam rail-motors, one-class only. They started at Cheltenham St James, reversing in both directions at Malvern Road. There they ran into a bay platform at the north end, tailor-made to accommodate the two coaches of the rail-motors. In later years, when the steam rail-motors were replaced by auto-trains with a small 0-4-2 tank engine at the north end of the train, the bay was not long enough as the engine did not clear the points giving access to the northbound line. Thereafter, the auto-trains used the southbound platform in both directions, where they reversed and there was a starting signal for 'wrong-line' working at the north end for the crossover to the northbound line.

All GWR local trains were hauled by tank engines between Cheltenham St James and Gloucester, and on the Kingham line. They were invariably 2-4-0Ts and looked very small in front of a GWR 70ft bogie carriage. Latterly, the 2-4-0Ts were superseded by 2-6-2Ts. Engines were always changed at Gloucester which was the main GWR shed. From the point of view of Cheltenham travellers, Gloucester has always been a cause of delay because all London trains in each direction

reversed there. On many trains, the Cheltenham portion was shunted across the station to join up with a Hereford via Ross portion, the London 4-6-0 engine being attached at what had been the rear end from Cheltenham. Arriving from London, it was not so bad, as the tank engine backed on to the rear of the train to reverse and then proceeded to Cheltenham.

Subsequently, the railway from Lansdown Junction, Cheltenham to Barnwood Junction, Gloucester has been reduced to two tracks and the old MR line through Eastgate station to Tuffley Junction has been lifted. The previous four-track section (two GW and two MR lines from Tuffley Junction to Standish Junction) has been reduced to two lines and a double junction laid in at Standish Junction to divert Swindon trains from the unrestricted Bristol route.

***Above left:*** **On the then four-track Gloucester–Cheltenham line, '5101' 2-6-2T No 4141 approaches Cheltenham in August 1950.** *B. Canning*

***Left:*** **Old memories stirred at Cheltenham Lansdown on 6 May 1956. Former Midland '2' 4-4-0s, Nos 40489/454, head a southbound rail tour.** *P. H. Wells*

***Above:*** **Cheltenham St James' station, 17 September 1960. From the left, '5101' 2-6-2T No 4116 on the 1.25pm to Gloucester, SR 'U' 2-6-0 No 31619 on the 1.48 pm to Southampton Terminus and a '57xx' 0-6-0PT on pilot duties.** *L. Sandler*

***Below:*** **SR 'U' 2-6-0 No 31620 leaves Cheltenham St James' on an Andover train c 1960.** *John C. Baker*

***Left:* '94xx' 0-6-0PT No 9453 on a Cheltenham–Kingham pick-up goods leaves Andoversford in January 1962.** *B. J. Ashworth*

***Below left:* 'Grange' 4-6-0 No 6855 *Saighton Grange* approaches Cheltenham on the Stratford line with the 06.55 Saturdays Wolverhampton Low Level-Penzance train of 31 July 1965.** *B. J. Ashworth*

***Right:* Class 50 No 50.030 (then un-named) stands in Cheltenham's surviving station (Lansdown) with a West Country–Liverpool express on 22 May 1974.** *Barry J. Nicolle*

All trains calling at Gloucester now use the old GW station's down platform extended at the east end to take two trains. There is a centre line with intermediate crossovers to allow independent use of the two halves of the platform. The result is that all Birmingham to Bristol line trains in both direction have to reverse in Gloucester station and the engine has to run round the train, except for certain trains which avoid Gloucester by running direct between Barnwood Junction and Gloucester South Junction.

The Cheltenham to Swindon trains are, except for two morning up trains and two evening down trains, which run through between Paddington and Cheltenham, diesel multiple-units mostly between Swindon, Cheltenham and Worcester and connect at Swindon with Inter-City 125 services at Swindon.

From Cheltenham's point of view, when BR remodelled the railways in the Gloucester area in the 1960s/1970s, Eastgate was the wrong station to be closed. When Eastgate was still in use, it was possible for all trains from both the Bristol and London directions to use this station and proceed to Cheltenham and the north without reversing, similarly in the opposite direction. Of course, the three level crossings over main streets in Gloucester were intolerable in modern traffic conditions. But once the former MR route was closed, it would have been perfectly possible from Barnwood Junction to beyond Stroud Road to build a high-level line on a viaduct with a station at the site of Eastgate. Four level crossings would have been eliminated for only a fraction of the cost of a motorway intersection such as Spaghetti Junction. As it is, the pernicious habit of reversing trains at the remodelled ex-GWR Gloucester Central station has been much extended to Birmingham to Bristol trains in both directions.

This account would not be complete without recording the engines found on Midland/LMS trains in the old days. The MR had no passenger engines bigger than the '990' class simples or Compound 4-4-0s and in MR days these were never sent down the Biriminghan to Bristol line. The principal expresses were almost invariably hauled by Johnson Class '3' 4-4-0s of the '700' series and the lesser trains by Class '2' 4-4-0s. Sometimes these trains were double headed with one of the lovely 4-2-2 'Spinners' and these could also be found solo on light trains. Stopping trains often had MR 2-4-0s. The LMS built more of the Compound 4-4-0s, known as 'Crimson Ramblers' and these took over the expresses, only in time to be superseded by 'Black Fives' and 'Jubilees'. There was one oddity in the form of a Great Malvern/Tewkesbury – Ashchurch train, hauled by an MR 0-4-4T. This was extended to Cheltenham, presumably to make connection with several southbound expresses and, possibly, with the Midland & South Western Junction train to Southampton. The train returned from Cheltenham at 1.30pm. The M&SWJR

engines worked that Company's four trains to and from Cheltenham Midland. They were 4-4-0s with small driving wheels; engines and carriages were painted in Midland red livery. Neither the MR nor the LSWR showed any desire to buy up the MSWJR and the result was that in the Grouping of railways in 1923 to form the Big Four, by reason of its geographical position the MSWJR became absorbed in the GWR who did its best to kill the line.

Another interesting working in the Cheltenham area was the Great Western and Great Central 'Ports to Ports Express' from Swansea to Newcastle via Banbury. The train avoided Cheltenham by using the Hatherley Curve and called at Cheltenham South and Leckhampton. It was generally hauled by 'Bulldog' 4-4-0s or by 'Aberdare' 2-6-0s suitable for the route through the Cotswold Hills.

Now, alas, St James and Malvern Road stations are closed and the Honeybourne, Hatherley Curve, M&SWJ and Kingham lines are all lifted.

***Right:* An IC125 unit eases into Cheltenham station on 22 March 1982. The train is the 08.20 Plymouth–Leeds.** *Les Bertram*

# Doncaster – 'near Swinton'

## D. L. Franks

ON 21 October 1948, the *Sheffield Evening Star* carried a news item with the above heading. I was the contributor. The feature read as follows:

> Less than 100 years ago, Doncaster, flourishing railway centre of today, was 'near Swinton' for purposes of railway travel.
>
> For several years after Swinton had been included in the North Midland network, anyone wishing to reach or leave Doncaster by the 'modern way of travel' had to make the journey between Doncaster and Swinton by horse-drawn coach.
>
> Swinton was on the line connecting Derby, Chesterfield, Masborough and Normanton to reach Leeds. Ninety-nine years ago Doncaster was linked to Swinton by the South Yorkshire Railway Company.
>
> The SYR had no locomotives, and these had to be supplied by other companies. Two years later, the Company extended its track from Mexborough to Barnsley, and also via Birdwell

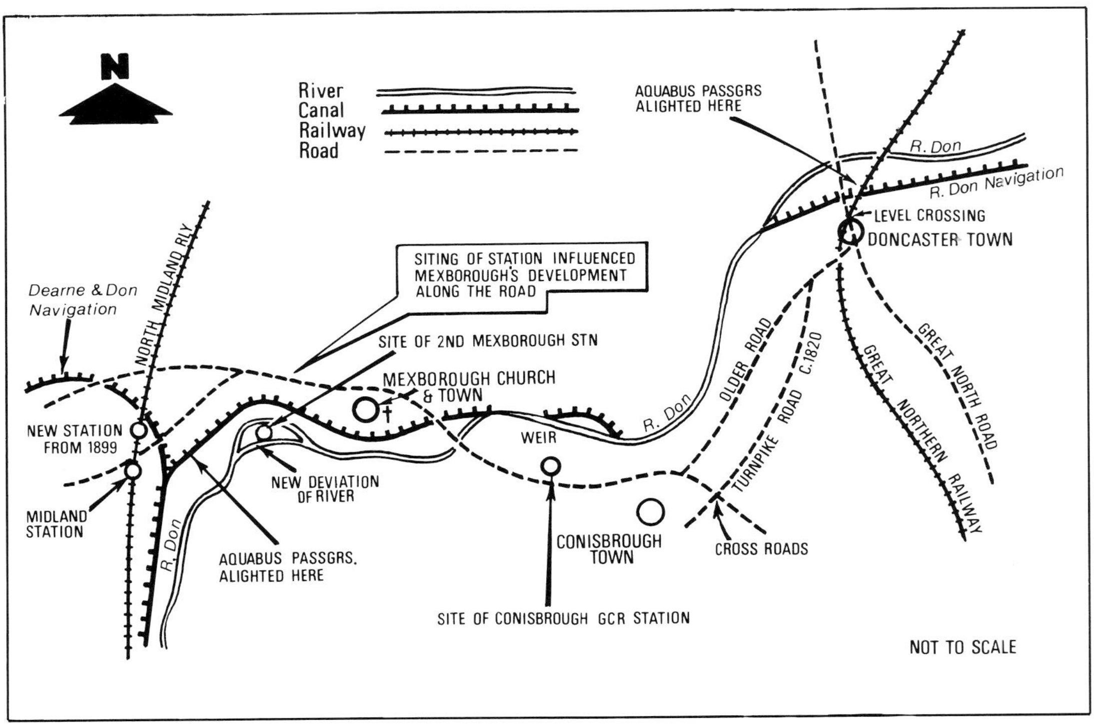


***Above:*** **Rail, road, canal and river in the Swinton and Doncaster area showing the route of the Aquabus.**

***Right:*** **North Midland Aquabus advertisement, 1841.** *Courtesy D. L. Franks*

and Meadow Hall to connect with the Rotherham and Sheffield Railway.

In the same year, Doncaster was connected to the Great Northern Railway system, by which time the local network was quickly taking shape.

The South Yorkshire Railway existed as a separate concern only for 15/16 years, until its merger in 1864 with the Manchester, Sheffield and Lincolnshire Railway, predecessor of the Great Central Railway and LNER system.

The third paragraph is not 100% true, yet conveyed to newspaper readers the idea that early railways were still, in 1849, rather primitive. The truer picture was that the SYR had *few* engines, not enough to work a passenger service; that was done by the Midland Railway – the former North Midland – from Sheffield to Doncaster. In simple fact, Midland passenger trains continued to run to Doncaster until World War 2, with goods services still longer. The Midland Railway owned a goods depot at Doncaster.

So much for background. During the period between the opening of the North Midland and the South Yorkshire Railway in November 1849, the station on the North Midland at Swinton was the most convenient for journeys west and north, and to London. For a slightly shorter period, journeys to and from Doncaster, west and north, were provided by the Lancashire and Yorkshire Railway, which had its first 'Doncaster' station at Arksey, and later a temporary one north of the present-day station. Prospective passengers from and to Doncaster had to seek means to connect with the North Midland at Swinton. The first service was by road-coach, but enterprising entrepreneurs devised the 'Aquabus', as portrayed in the hand-bill shown. Distances were not so significant in those hard days for town journeys. This is evident in the case of the 'booking office' of the *White Bear Inn*, the actual point of departure of the 'Aquabus' being nearly half a mile away. There was another walk of 300–400 yards or so at Swinton to reach the station.

The hand-bill dated 9 March 1841 was followed by a similar one dated 30 April 1842, but this is not in the possession of the writer.

**DONCASTER AND SWINTON.**

THE AQUABUS leaves SWINTON STATION for DONCASTER every Morning, Sundays excepted, on the arrival of the down train which leaves Derby at Six, Sheffield at Half-past Seven, and the up train which leaves Leeds at a Quarter-past Seven.

Again leaves the MILL BRIDGE, Doncaster, for Swinton, in the Afternoon at One o'clock, to meet the down train to Leeds, York, Hull, and Manchester, and the up train to Sheffield, Derby, &c.

Fares,—Best Cabin, 1s.—Fore Cabin, 9d.

For particulars apply at the WHITE BEAR INN, Doncaster.

N.B. POST HORSES on the shortest Notice.

*Swinton, March 9, 1841.*

# By the seaside

British railways led to creation of our modern seaside resorts, as well as providing many an attractive scene as railway lines skirt the seashore.

***Far left:*** **At least a few of the holidaymakers at St Ives seem to have noticed the appearance of this Lelant Saltings–St Ives diesel multiple-unit formation nearing its terminus on 9 July 1981.**
*Brian Morrison*

***Left:*** **The clocktower at Cleethorpes station seems very appropriate for a holiday resort . . . but it does show that the Class 114 unit forming the 15.47 for New Holland Pier was late on leaving . . . 24 May 1980.** *Brian Morrison*

***Below:*** **Seaside stations should mean lots of passengers – such as this queue at Skegness waiting to join a Grantham train in August 1981.**
*Kevin Lane*

*Above:* **Steam beside the coast . . . the return 'Cumbrian Coast Express' from Maryport is seen near Nethertown, south of Whitehaven, headed by 'Duchess' 4-6-2 No 46229 *Duchess of Hamilton* on 11 August 1982.** *L. A. Nixon*

*Right:* **Holidaymakers board the 13.06 to Exeter St Davids at Exmouth on 14 July 1982.** *Brian Morrison*

# Ffestiniog spring

## Jim Palm

FOR SOMEONE who normally plans well in advance, the decision to go to North Wales was very much a last-minute one. Thirty minutes of frenzied phoning sorted out the arrangements. 'You've left it rather late,' chided one Porthmadog landlady, 'But we can always find room for people connected with the railway.' How did she know? Or did the steam coming out of her earpiece give the game away?

When the 13.00 Holyhead train drew silently out of Euston on Monday, 24 May 1982, I was settled comfortably on board and responded very quickly to the call for lunch which came from the loudspeaker up above me. Settled equally comfortably in the restaurant car, I was looking forward to tomato soup and grilled fillets of haddock served with parsley potatoes, garden peas and carrots, followed by apple and blackberry pie with cream, the whole lot being washed down with a pint of ice-cold lager. As I mused in my corner seat, my mouth quietly watering, I was aware of a liveried attendant hovering uncertainly. 'I'm sorry, sir,' he mumbled apologetically, 'You're reading the wrong menu.' Ah well, I supposed it would be Coke and a sausage roll after all. As it turned out, the substitute menu was equally appetising and I left the table overwhelmingly replete. In other words, I ate too much.

We were to arrive half an hour late at Llandudno Junction, which mattered little since had we been on schedule, there would have been a 60-minute wait for the Conwy Valley line train. I still had time for light refreshments and got chatting to a charming

**_Below:_ Hunslet 2-4-0TT _Blanche_ on an engineer's train becomes the first Ffestiniog Railway steam locomotive to reach the new Blaenau Ffestiniog Central station, having accompanied the first BR passenger train to arrive, 22 March 1982.** _FR Co_

young lady in the station buffet. It turned out that she ran a Post Office and general store up in the hills and was on her way home after spending the weekend in London. 'I managed to buy my eldest the new Depeché Mode in Oxford Street,' she said. 'Oh good,' I enthused, having not the slightest idea what she was talking about. 'I hope it fits.' She looked at me as though I was mad and returned to her cup of tea.

As the local train made its way up the Conwy Valley, the clouds descended and it grew noticeably darker. What looked like an albatross circled ominously overhead, eyeing our train with suspicion. I was just telling my Depeché Mode companion one of my favourite railway ghost stories when, with a blast on the horn, we rumbled into the dank gloom of the two-mile Ffestiniog Tunnel, itself reputed to be haunted. The dark shape lurking in the shadows turned out to be a travelling ticket inspector who tripped over my bag, staggered irretrievably and sat down rather heavily on somebody's feet. Cursing forcibly in Welsh he got up, looked at me with undisguised malevolence and stomped off down the train.

Soon we were grinding to a halt at the new Blaenau Ffestiniog Central station. I gathered up my things, took leave of the lady from the hills and headed for the hotel. I was greeted by about 200 children which spoke well for the fertility of the Welsh but made it hard to understand what my host was saying. In this sadly depressed town, the café adjoining was apparently the only place for youngsters to go for an evening. Space Invaders seemed a better idea than smashing shop windows although it appeared later that some managed to find time for both. My hosts made me more than welcome. Having made my mark in the visitors' book, I was ushered upstairs, shown the television lounge and brought to a halt on the landing. 'I've put you in here,' announced my guide, throwing open a door. 'Mmm,' I remarked, 'It's a bit small.' I didn't really fancy spending the night in the lavatory. 'Oh, I'm sorry,' gasped the landlady, 'How silly of me. We've only just moved in and I don't quite know my way around.' We finally settled for Bedroom No 1 in which I was to spend a very comfortable night; there was only one snag, I couldn't lock the door. I don't carry a small kit of tools for nothing and, having fixed the lock, it took me half an hour to get out the next morning.

Having freshened myself up after arrival, a breath of air seemed a good idea so I walked back into the town to inspect the new joint station. The first Ffestiniog Railway train would be steaming in the following morning and this was the reason for my visit. There were very few people about, posssibly because it was growing dark and had begun to rain. As I came back across the new footbridge, I passed two men trying to erect a banner in something approaching a Force Ten gale, drenching rain now sweeping down from the mist-clad hills. Blaenau's High Street was understandably deserted, apart

***Right:*** **FR Double Fairlie *Merddin Emrys* at the head of a nine-coach train breasts the steepest gradient on the FR's main line to approach the new Blaenau Ffestiniog Central station in June 1982.** *FR Co*

from the occasional Crosville bus and youngsters huddled in doorways munching chips. A solitary motorcyclist zoomed past me, the words Black Sabbath emblazoned across the back of his leather jacket, and spluttered to a halt fifty yards ahead. When I reached him he was crouching on all fours, peering into the works. 'What's up?' I asked, trying to look knowledgeable. 'Water's got in the engine, I think,' he replied, endeavouring to swear and succeeding brilliantly. 'Oh,' I added helpfully, 'It's getting into your helmet, too.' He glanced down at his space-age headgear, inverted on the kerb and slowly filling with rain. As he began to swear forcefully again I handed him a toffee, wished him luck, and moved on.

The big day dawned anything but bright and clear. It was cold, windy and very wet. I tucked into a hearty breakfast, bracing myself for the worst that the Welsh mountain weather could produce. On arriving at the station well before 10am nothing was happening and scarcely a soul was to be seen, so I retired to the café across the road for further refreshment. I can't understand how anyone can tuck into iced buns and sticky doughnuts at that hour, I made do with some fresh cream cakes and a slice or two of fruit tart.

Back at the station, the pace was soon hotting up and people had appeared from nowhere, jamming the footbridge and covering every square inch of platform. I bumped into enthusiast Robert Symes, not long retired from the BBC and aghast at my being let loose on the railway; his actual comment is unrepeatable. Peter Wood of the Ffestiniog Railway Society's London Area Group arrived resplendent in a super-high visibility anorak. This prompted me to dig into my bag and don my orange vest – at least it made me look official. The trouble was that it refused to fit properly over my clothes and kept riding up around my neck, threatening to choke me. To everyone's regret this didn't happen and I positioned myself beside the track just outside the station, along with photographers and general sightseers to await the first narrow gauge train. On these occasions I always curse people who insist on milling about near my microphones and I viewed with concern an elderly man who began to do just that. Even worse, he insisted on talking. In the ordinary way, I chat with anyone but, when about to make a recording, my lips are sealed and I wish to heaven that everyone else could be silenced, too. Having discussed the weather, the crowds and the state of his corns he asked whether he was in my way. 'No,' I replied, 'But please don't talk because I'm about to make a recording.'

'What of?', he wanted to know. 'The train that's coming in a few minutes,' I explained. 'Whatever for?' he went on, fidgeting uncomfortably – I think his corns were troubling him. 'It's an historic moment,' I said, peering anxiously down the track and willing him to go away. 'Are you local?' he asked, eyeing me up and down. Did I sound as though I was local? 'No,' I sighed, 'I'm from London.' He stared at me in utter disbelief. 'From London?' he gasped. 'You're from London? And you've come all this way just to record a train? I don't believe it. I simply don't believe it!' He backed away from the mad Englishman who had travelled 250 miles just to record a steam train. At least it would give him something to tell his grandchildren. 'Actually,' he confided, having overcome his initial shock, 'I'm looking for a hole in the fence; I want to get out.' This was the best news I had heard all day; I'd been hoping he would find a hole in the ground and disappear down it. As the train approached, he actually wandered off and I was able to record its arrival unmolested.

Double Fairlie *Earl of Merioneth* was at the head of the first FR passenger train into Blaenau Ffestiniog since 1939 and it seemed as though the whole of North Wales had turned out to witness the event. Somehow the rain had managed to hold off for an hour or two but, with the train in at the platform and special guests being urged to climb aboard for the run back to Porthmadog, the gods stopped smiling and the heavens opened. They remained open for the rest of the day. I made the trip that afternoon, consuming en route a modest Ffestiniog packed lunch and an enormous freelance Eccles cake. '*I* didn't have one of those,' pouted the man in the next seat as we whistled our way through Tan-y-Bwlch. 'Where did you get it from?' 'Eccles,' was all I could say.

With several interviews safely in the can, the train steamed into Porthmadog. Passengers made a beeline for the buffet and the station shop did a brisk trade in souvenirs. And still the rain came down. That evening, I appeared to be the only person walking across the Cob. This may have been because it was nearly dark, blowing hard and raining even harder. My umbrella turned inside-out so many times that in the end I left it that way.

It was still raining the next morning when I boarded the BR train for the journey back to London. Seated at the front of the diesel multiple-unit, I was soon chatting with the driver, who was from Machynlleth. Our conversation turned to farming, the state of the economy, the weather and flexible rostering. As we trundled rhythmically on, he told me he was looking forward to his lunch. 'The wife does a lovely bit of haddock,' he said, staring dreamily down the track. Ah! Grilled haddock with parsley potatoes, garden peas and carrots, followed by apple and blackberry pie with fresh cream; the whole lot washed down, of course, with a pint of ice-cold lager. The thought of it made feel ravenous and I burrowed in my bag to see what I could find.

I had to settle for Coke and a sausage roll. Of course.

# 60 years ago

Our photo-feature, by courtesy of Rail Archive Stephenson, reviews the scene at the southern end of the Great Northern main line in 1924, showing how the newly formed London and North Eastern Railway was making its mark by new liveries and with the transfer of locomotives from other constituent companies.

***Above:*** **Four-cylinder 'C1' 4-4-2 No 3279 passes Greenwood with the 5.10 pm King's Cross–Doncaster slow train, summer 1924. An 'O2' 2-8-0 waits to take the double track section through to Potters Bar.** *F.R. Hebron/Rail Archive Stephenson*

***Above right:*** **'K3' 2-6-0 No 1002, in GNR livery, approaches Wood Green with a lengthy up goods, including a number of fish vans.** *F. R. Hebron/Rail Archive Stephenson*

***Right:*** **'Al' 4-6-2 No 1481N, as yet un-named, heads the 1.30 pm King's Cross–Leeds/Bradford through Oakleigh Park. The 'N' suffix denoted GNR group locomotives.** *F.R. Hebron/Rail Archive Stephenson*

1002

3252

***Top left:*** **The coming of the LNER led to the introduction of Pullman car expresses into/out of King's Cross. This is the up 'Sheffield Pullman', near Cemetery Box, late on a summer evening. The engine is 'C1' 4-4-2 No 4461.** *F. R. Hebron/Rail Archive Stephenson*

***Left:*** **Ivatt 'C2' 4-4-2 No 3252 under easy steam, having emerged from Hadley South Tunnel with a Hunstanton–King's Cross restaurant car express. The train is made up of former Great Eastern corridor stock, except for the brake coaches at either end which are North Eastern Railway design vehicles, built for the GE section by the LNER.** *F. R. Hebron/Rail Archive Stephenson*

***Top:*** **Nowadays, the GN main line sees very little goods traffic at its southern end, whereas 60 years ago it was host to lengthy coal (and empties) trains. A short, mixed goods heads north on the slow lines near Greenwood behind 'O2' 2-8-0 No 490N in the spring of 1924.**
*F. R. Hebron/Rail Archive Stephenson*

***Above:*** **Fascinating! Next to 'D2' 4-4-0 No 1391, waiting for the road at Greenwood, is one of the ex-GNR orchid vans, by now LNER No 964N.**
*F. R. Hebron/Rail Archive Stephenson*

***Left:*** **The 'N2' 0-6-2Ts were beginning to appear in quantity on GN suburban trains and were to displace many of the earlier 'N1' engines. No 1570 of the latter in non-standard livery is whiling away the time at Finsbury Park when engaged on Alexandra Palace branch duties.** *F. R. Hebron/Rail Archive Stephenson*

***Above right:*** **The LNER began to draft in 'N7' 0-6-2Ts of Great Eastern Railway inspiration, such as No 995E, leaving Wood Green in the autumn of 1924 with the 11.05 am King's Cross–Hatfield. Early non-corridor bogie of Howlden design behind the engine, followed by two Gresley lavatory articulated twins.** *F R. Hebron/Rail Archive Stephenson*

***Right:*** **Great Northern metals also saw former North London trains with suburban passenger workings to/from Broad Street. Resplendent in the early LMS crimson lake livery, ex-NLR 4-4-0T, LMS No 6462, waits outside Finsbury Park with a train for Broad Street.** *F. R. Hebron/Rail Archive Stephenson*

***Above:*** **Former Great Eastern Railway express locomotives began to appear on the GN, too. 'D15' 4-4-0 No 1872E leaves Hadley Wood South Tunnel with the up royal train from Wolferton to King's Cross conveying King George V and Queen Mary, 3 November 1924.**
*F. R. Hebron/Rail Archive Stephenson*

***Below:*** **Premier ex-Great Central motive power worked into King's Cross after Grouping. 'B3' 4-6-0 No 1169, still in GCR livery, passes Greenwood, south of Hadley Wood, with the up 'Flying Scotsman' in the summer of 1924.**
*F. R. Hebron/Rail Archive Stephenson*

# An American's introduction to the Gricer

Drena Hills

IF YOU were to look up 'Gricer' in an American dictionary, (yes, the American language actually warrants a dictionary), it wouldn't be there.

The closest thing you might come across would be a 'Train Watcher' which, while more descriptive, lacks the possibilities of the word Gricer.

I came face to face with them when I visited England for the time with a Britrail Pass, an idea sensibly devised to keep Americans off British roads.

There really should be some kind of warning attached to it, because it can be a terrifying experience to come across a coach full of gricers without advance knowledge of what to expect.

I first became aware of something peculiar when I stepped on to the platform at Paddington one Saturday morning, bound for Cardiff. I had to wait for a friend and as I did I became aware that there was something fascinating about the front of the train.

People would hurry down, take a picture, write something in a notebook and board the train. Some just wrote in a notebook. Curiosity overcame me and I wandered down to see what I was missing.

There was nothing to see, but I was to learn better later.

The coach was filled to capacity and we found ourselves opposite two boys no more than ten or eleven years old. They were bent over a small book, studying it intently and my first thought was they were catching up on homework.

Again, I should have known better. Ten year old boys are a universal product and none, whether English or American, does homework on a Saturday – at least not without threats of violence.

The train started and all was peaceful for about 20 seconds. Suddenly, there was a flash of activity similar only to a German U-boat being spotted by a British patrol ship. Numbers were called out and mass scribbling went on around me until I felt out of place.

I stared out of the window to see what I had missed. All I could see were three or four locomotives disappearing into the distance.

I looked back as one of the boys sighed happily. 'I needed that '47'.'

***Below:*** **BREL Doncaster Works yard is under inspection by a trainload of Gricers, on 19 August 1979. Examples of Classes 03,31,37,50,55 and 56 are the subject of interest.** *Brian Morrison*

True, I am near-sighted, but I could hardly have missed 47 of anything, especially 47 things so obviously breathtaking that they stirred the entire train to action.

I looked back at the two boys who were huddled once more over the ever-mysterious, clearly indispensable notebook.

'Hi,' I said. (I have found the English never say 'Hi', but it's a sure method of getting attention).

'Hello,' the one by the window answered back and I wasn't sure if the greeting, or the accent startled him more.

'What on earth are you doing?'

Blunt, but a sure approach.

'I missed that '08'.'

My friend gave up and went back to her book, confiding later she thought it was a mental home on a field trip.

Determined I pressed on.

'What are those numbers?'

***Above:*** **Gricers in action as a rail tour headed by Class 33 No 33.107 with Class 491 push-pull sets and buffet car visit North Woolwich on 11 March 1978.**
*Brian Morrison*

'You mean *train* numbers?' 'We write down the numbers of the trains we see, I'm a train spotter,' his friend said proudly. 'Don't you have them in America?'

'No, we're a deprived nation, what's the prize?', I asked, leafing through the book I was handed.

'Prize?'

I should have realised. The English are far more civilised. An American rarely sees a reason for anything that doesn't end up in dollars and cents.

'We ride on the trains and try to get all the numbers in the book.'

*The* book – it was said with awe and respect – listed every single locomotive on British Rail.

'Oh, when you're going places.'

'Oh, no!'

'Let me get this straight, you don't ride to get anywhere?'

'No, we get off at a station and then wait on the platforms to get more numbers,' he said with a sigh that indicated heaven was very close to a train platform. 'Some people take pictures.'

That explained the cameras. 'Train-spotter, huh?'

'Gricer.'

'Gricer?'

'That's the official term.'

Gricer it was.

By the time we reached Cardiff I had received a crash-course in train-spotting, which was strange when you consider I still hadn't figured out how to read the train timetables.

Each type of locomotive (distinguished by the same front two numbers of its class) was of a different design. This made it no easier to tell them apart, even though my gricer friends could recognise the various shapes before they ever saw the numbers. Considering there were about 20 different classes I regarded this as quite a feat. I know gricers everywhere would cringe at the thought, but at the time it seemed that painting all the classes a different colour provided a far easier solution. Each locomotive belonged to a particular BR Region, though some got around everywhere. On the whole I came to the conclusion that astrophysics would be a less exacting hobby.

Few of us got off at Cardiff. Some unknown paradise called Swansea was the destination of most of the passengers.

On the way back I was once more next to a train-spotter, which isn't very hard to do. However, this one would turn out to be my future husband. Feeling more as though I belonged, I struck up a conversation. He wanted to know about American trains and I was sadly ignorant. Not the best of first impressions, but he marrried me anyway.

In fact, I had hardly ever been on a train. In Los Angeles we regarded them more as curiosities than as forms of transport.

After I married him five months later I began to wish I had paid more attention to railways.

Magical words like 'Southern Region', 'emus', and 'shunters' were to become part of my vocabulary.

Cities like Derby, York, Glasgow and Crewe became the most-favoured resorts.

Crewe is the Mecca of train spotting. The 'in-thing' is to sit on wet platforms. Station platforms are always wet and never have a place for you to sit. One would think that with the revenue brought in by gricers someone would have erected a couple of memorial benches here and there. The idea is to drink bad tea, eat sausage rolls and pounce on any – and all – trains of interest.

***Above:*** **Open Day at Laira depot, 25 April 1982. A crowd lays siege to the HST servicing shed.** *Charles F. Beatson*

***Above right:*** **The overbridge to the south of Doncaster station: limits to gricing – and some extraordinary notices!** *Kevin Lane*

Naturally all trains are of interest, even wrecked ones, which have the added fascination of mutilation going for them.

I first saw Crewe when we were to have a tour of the Works. There are two ways to get into a British Rail Engineering works. There are organised tours, for which you send away for tickets, and Open Days where everyone gets them at the door.

It's very important to get into one of the Works since it gives you the chance to wander around and see locomotives in states of disembowelment: being repaired, painted and sometimes scrapped. I was amazed that no matter how many damaged locomotives we saw no one ever got put off train travel.

Unfortunately, on our first trip we went by train. I say 'unfortunately' because no one had thought about the gricers and had built the works on the other side of town from the station.

I had been told it was just a short walk from the station and, being naïve, believed it. Never, ever believe an Englishman who tells you that something is a short walk. Short walks call for overnight bags and canteens. 'Just around the corner' is cause enough for endurance training and the heartless announcement of 'We're almost there', simply translated means, 'Buck up lad, only another 20 miles'.

Not that scenery takes your mind off it either. On first acquaintance, Crewe is not breathtaking and it doesn't get any better closer at hand. On a Sunday, the town is a dreary place, devoid of life and human beings.

Once through the gates of the works you are

***Above:*** **Class 50 'Haulage' Gricers demonstrate their enthusiasm on the occasion when No 50.042 worked to and from Manchester Piccadilly, 12 September 1982. The '50' took a Paddington–Manchester train throughout, and is seen here at Longsight as it returned to Birmingham with the 16.15 to Cardiff.** *A. Sherratt*

deposited at the bicycle stand and told to wait for your guide. British Rail has a healthy respect for gricers and doesn't like to think what would happen if they were let loose.

After the trudge from the station you are then expected to walk around the entire works, (enthusiastically, of course), and then trek all the way back to the next train. That is always leaving in 15 minutes so it means a run back to the station.

If Britain had been able to send over gricers during the American Revolution we would be drinking tea still. Not only do they walk endless miles through appalling bouts of weather, but they can see numbers whizzing by at incredible speeds, remember them and write down half-a-dozen an hour later when they have the chance.

On a steady diet of British Rail tea – which I have nothing against, I'm just wary of liquids when my spoon floats on top of them – sausage rolls and nasty little boxed apple-pies, gricers are undaunted.

They follow strict rules in their pursuits, especially the photographers.

First and foremost, no train is ever too far away, or going too fast that it can't be caught . . . regardless of who or what is in the way.

If you come across a trail beaten out of bushes and bogs, defying nature, rivers and local zoning laws and it ends unexpectedly at a railway line, it was forged by a gricer.

Works Open Days are the best. They take on a carnival atmosphere and gricers who really do have families – and didn't spring into existence from a British Rail compartment – bring theirs along. Everyone wanders around, has a picnic lunch, drinks more of that 'tea' and generally enjoys themselves.

The 'tea' will always be an acquired taste for me – something like learning to imbibe cyanide, but healthier.

To add to the carnival atmosphere, people set up tables and sell train memorabilia which is totally irresistible. I have station signs for most of the civilised world, one a 5ft metal example from a place I've never heard of, headlamps that are so beautifully rusty that I haven't the heart to clean them and assorted other treasures that cheerfully clutter up our home. I honestly believe that if BR had a Class 33 locomotive in my price range I would have bought it by now!

The best part of a Works Open Day is that you are allowed to climb into locomotive cabs. It *is* possible to go into an Open Day feeling blasé, but once you have sat in the driver's seat and made an imaginary run to the far corners of the earth, you are hooked for life.

It is a well-known fact that every gricer would love the chance to be a driver, but it would never work. They would be forever ploughing into stations trying to get the number of the shunter that just passed a minute ago.

I learned that the saddest part of being a gricer was the withdrawal of not merely a particular locomotive, but an entire class. For all my sincere attention, I could only ever recognise one class without difficulties and that was the 'Deltics'; these were what they called locomotives beginning with the numbers '55'. My knowledge came from sketching one and coming to know it backwards and forwards. Naturally, British Rail scrapped the entire class. I became indignant and then a little sad.

It was then I realised that the worst had happened – I was turning into a gricer.

What would my mother have said?

True, it will be a long time before I can stand for hours in a snowdrift waiting for that elusive Class 27. Or be able to tell the difference between a Class 25 and a 26 without pausing. Or even get more than one set of numbers as we whiz by a station. But all is not lost: at least now I can read timetables.

But I don't think I'll ever get used to that tea.

# Through the viewfinder

These four pages feature the work of photographer G. W. Osborne and present a variety of usual – and less usual – workings from the last few years of WR steam.

***Above:*** **'Castles' were in their last days of featuring on the Paddington–Worcester– Hereford service in the spring of 1964. However, this is the Oxford University Railway Society special of 6 May 1964 which took No 5054 *Earl of Ducie* to Hereford. The train emerges from Ledbury Tunnel.**

*Left:* By the end of 1962 this service had been withdrawn. Ivatt '2' 2-6-0 No 46401 near Marteg Halt, north of Rhayader, with the 12.45 pm Builth Road–Moat Lane Junction of 13 April 1962.

*Below:* The Hereford–Gloucester service lasted until 1964, and was mostly steam worked until the end. Having crossed an eastbound train, '43xx' 2-6-0 No 7335 pulls away from Mitcheldean Road station at the head of the 2.30 pm Gloucester–Hereford on 22 June 1963.

*Right:* 'English Electric' Type 3 (now Class 37) No D6607 comes alongside for a look at '45xx' 2-6-2T No 4555 and '14xx' 0-4-2T No 1420. Both were fresh from attention at Worcester Works and were on their way south to new pastures on the Dart Valley Railway in October 1965.

*Below:* Early days of inter-Regional diesel working: BRCW Type 3 No D6549 (now Class 33) eases past Worcester shed with a Fawley-Bromford Bridge oil train in the spring of 1963.

*Above:* Evidence that 'Royal Scots' penetrated the Worcester–Hereford line, at least as far as Malvern Wells. No 46100 *Royal Scot,* of Saltley shed, on what would appear to be a train from Birmingham New St, at Malvern Wells on 24 June 1961.

*Below:* Southampton FC's activity in the FA Cup during the 1962/63 season brought SR Pacifics to the West Midlands on specials. Rebuilt 'West Country' 4-6-2 No 34046 *Braunton* and green-painted SR train lend unusual atmosphere to Worcester Tunnel Junction in April 1963, en route to Birmingham.

# Incident at Maiden Newton

## Ken Cole

TO SOME people, being a railway enthusiast may mean nothing more than simply watching trains, but others take a close interest in other things such as stations and signalling. There is also a 'social' dimension to being an enthusiast. As well as meeting others of a like mind, the enthusiast cannot fail to come into contact with members of the railway staff.

I have nearly always found that a considerate and friendly attitude towards railway staff will get a friendly reception in return. Indeed, over the years it has been a pleasure to meet hundreds of railwaymen (and women) whose paths have crossed mine, both professionally and as an enthusiast. However, in an organisation employing thousands there are bound to be exceptions. Occasionally there is someone who views all enthusiasts with disdain. I encountered one such individual when visiting Maiden Newton, in Dorset.

Maiden Newton had once been a busy junction on the main line from Castle Cary to Weymouth. With the closure of the connecting branch to Bridport, the former main line had been reduced to single track, and nowadays the station is little more than a slumbering wayside halt.

Driving up the steep approach to the station, I noticed the impressive red-brick arch carrying the railway over a minor road, together with the unusual knapped-flint station buildings and the iron fence across the goods yard.

I pulled up in the station yard. Opposite me was the familiar sight of a slate-roofed brick-built Great Western Railway signal cabin. Down the line I noticed a lower-quadrant semaphore signal. At the

end of the platform was a rare survival: an old cattle dock, complete with its siding. If it wasn't for the intruding modern signs, the scene could almost have been from the 1950s rather than the 1980s. It was, I decided, well-worth taking a closer look, and perhaps a few photographs as well.

As I got out from the car and entered what I had thought was a deserted station, I was surprised to see an oldish, stocky man in railway uniform hurrying by on the platform. 'You going up or down?' he called out rather abruptly. In answer, I said that I had only come to look at the station. 'There's nothing to see here!' he retorted, to which I replied that there seemed to be quite a lot to interest me.

After this brief exchange the man continued on his way, over the timber crossing and up into the signalbox. My rather cold reception was a disappointment, since on numerous previous visits to such places I found the signalmen (or 'bobbies' as they are known) both friendly and helpful. Faced with the unfriendly attitude of this particular bobby, I would have to forget any thoughts of investigating the 'box' and content myself with exploring the station instead.

After having a quick look round, I returned to the car to get my camera. I decided to take a photograph of the signalbox from the cattle dock. Just at that moment another car pulled into the station yard and parked right on the edge of the dock, completely blocking my hoped-for picture.

Undaunted, I approached the offending vehicle and politely asked its driver if he would mind moving it for a moment so that I could take a photograph. The driver was amiable, and readily consented to move his car out of the way. This was done and I was just about to take my picture when the wooden window of the signalbox suddenly slid open.

'Have you got permission to take photographs?' a gruff voice demanded. The signalman's face, peering down from the box, looked grim. I replied that so far as I was aware it was not normally necessary to obtain permission to take photographs from those parts of a station open to the public. In case he felt I had no right to be there, I would be quite happy to purchase a platform ticket.

This remark seemed to have a surprising effect. The man lost his temper and almost fell over as he shouted out that he didn't sell platform tickets! With that, he retreated back into his box and slammed the window shut.

I assumed that would be the end of the matter, and proceeded to take my picture. However, no sooner had I sqeezed the camera shutter than the window shot open again and a voice came bellowing across the tracks: 'I don't want my picture taken!'.

Rather taken aback by this amazing outburst, it

***Left:*** **The tranquility of Maiden Newton is disturbed by the departure of the 18.00 Weymouth–Bristol, leaving the station on 13 June 1981.** *Les Bertram*

***Right:*** **The Dorset countryside receives the diesel fumes of Class 31 No 31.193, leaving Maiden Newton with the 10.05 Weymouth–Bristol of 2 September 1976.** *Les Bertram*

soon occurred to me that there was an obvious reply to such a blunt statement. 'If you don't want your picture taken, all you have to do is get back inside and close the window', I called out with unquestionable logic.

The signalman glared down from his lofty perch, and seemed to be foaming at the mouth. Presumably he had a grudge against railway enthusiasts, in particular those with cameras! No doubt someone with a camera had upset him on a previous occasion, but that gave him no right to take it out on me. He was in the wrong and he probably knew it. Whatever happened, I was determined not to let him intimidate me.

Then the man fired his next broadside: 'We don't want so and so photographers running all over the place. What we need is passengers to travel on the railway'.

This is a sentiment with which I would wholeheartedly agree. However, it was inappropriate because I was certainly not running about. His implication that I didn't travel by train was unfounded. Although on this occasion I had arrived by car, little did he know that I had also travelled as a fare-paying passenger over virtually every railway line in the country.

The signalman continued raving: 'You've got a cheek, ordering our passengers out of the way so you can take your damn pictures!'.

In an effort to restore some calm to the situation, I pointed out that I had not ordered the car driver out of the way at all; I had merely made a polite request with which the gentleman had complied, although he was not compelled to do so. However, the signalman was not impressed by this argument, he hadn't finished his attack. 'You come here and run all over the tracks! You're a danger to yourselves and to the public!' he roared.

This was really going too far: my feet had remained firmly on the platform and I wasn't endangering anyone. Of course, some railway enthusiasts do behave in an irresponsible fashion, but that was no reason to assume that anyone with a camera would act in the same way. It obviously didn't occur to him that some visitors to his station might even be railwaymen, or ex-railwaymen themselves!

By now the adrenalin was beginning to flow, and I was becoming extremely angry. 'Who the hell do you think you are?' I called out. 'What right have you to shout abuse at someone who's just innocently taking pictures? Why do you assume I'm going to run across the tracks? You should ask first before you start shouting!'.

This seemed to leave him dumbfounded: instead of saying anything in reply, he retreated back into his box and slammed the window shut. A few seconds later, I went over to see the driver who had moved his car for me. 'I must apologise for that unpleasantness', I said, 'but the things he said were completely unjustified'.

'That's quite all right', said the car driver. 'You're right, he is a misery; he doesn't come from these parts, none of us around here know him. Blokes like him give the railway a bad name and discourage people from using the trains'.

Feeling gratified by this vindication of my own feelings, I smiled and thanked him once more for moving his car. Then I returned to the platforms and turned my attention to photographing the station buildings.

Five minutes later I noticed that, as if by magic, the station had suddenly started to come to life. There were now several cars parked in the yard, and people were milling about on the platforms in hushed expectancy. The lines to north and south were both single track, and looking at the timetable I saw that two trains were shortly due to pass each other at the station.

Soon I heard bells ringing in the signalbox, and the crash of the lever as the signalman pulled off the down home signal. I hoped that the man had recovered sufficiently from his earlier rage to enable him to operate his instruments in safety!

Then a diesel unit for Weymouth clattered around the corner, under the bridge and into the station. The train screeched to a halt and the doors slammed in unison. I went over to the other platform and stood waiting in anticipation for the Bristol train, which would appear in the distance at any moment. I decided to take a photograph of the two trains passing and had my camera at the ready. Meanwhile, a throng of people gathered around me, all peering intently at the horizon as if they were marooned at sea and their lives depended on it.

At last the levers crashed again, the up home signal dipped, and the faint rumble of a distant diesel locomotive started to grow louder. Then the door of the signalbox shut with a bang and the signalman strode across the timber crossing. In his hand was the large metal hoop containing the single line token for Yeovil, which he was about to give to the driver of the second train in exchange for the token from Dorchester.

I waited apprehensively as the man came up the platform ramp towards me, his face as grim as ever. I was still determined not to be intimidated, so my camera remained firmly in my hand. Was he going to start arguing again and cause me to miss my picture? Perhaps he might suddenly go mad and hit me over the head with the token, or even push me into the path of the oncoming train!

I needn't have worried. The signalman walked past with his eyes rigidly focused straight ahead, as if trying to pretend I wasn't there. Thirty seconds later, the big Class 47 diesel locomotive roared in, and the signalman exchanged tokens with the driver in the centre of the platform.

It occurred to me that this was rather unusual since the normal practice would have been to exchange the tokens at the platform end, opposite the signalbox. I wondered whether this was a deliberate ploy on the part of the signalman who, obstinate to the last, wanted to prevent me taking his photograph as the train came in!

Later, as I drove away from the station, I couldn't help feeling sorry for the signalman, despite his unwarranted attack. There was a grain of truth in his opinion of photographers. Although he was obviously prejudiced, no doubt his prejudices had been fuelled by irresponsible behaviour on the part of some previous visitor. Certainly there are plenty of 'nutters' around who think nothing of 'running all over the tracks' taking snapshots, and who never travel by train themselves.

But the more I thought about it, the more I was puzzled by the signalman's hostile behaviour. Even if some idiot had upset him on a previous occasion, surely no normal person would be quite so aggressive just because someone happened to have a camera? I wondered whether there might be another reason. Perhaps his wife had just left him, or he had just been made redundant.

A a few weeks later, and quite by chance, the mystery was solved. My attention was caught by an item in the *Radio Times* about an episode of the tv series *To the Manor Born (Cookham* or *Hinton* perhaps?). It concerned a railway station threatened with closure.

Tuning in to the programme, I was astonished to see the snobbish Audrey Fforbes-Hamilton talking down to the 'Station Master' in front of those same unusual, knapped-flint station buildings, thinly disguised as 'Malbury'. Later scenes featured her standing on the platform with about a dozen tv 'extras' busily going about their various roles, while trains came and went.

The filming must have taken several days; putting two and two together, I could imagine the signalman's patience being sorely tried as cameramen swarmed across the tracks and the director called for the train to be returned to the platform for yet another 'take' of its departure. I wondered just how many arguments there had been between the film crew and the signalman!

Assuming that this is what actually happened, the signalman's attitude towards photographers could be understood, even if there was still no excuse for it. If he ever hears this story, then I hope he will realise that some people do have the sense not to run around making a nuisance of themselves. After all, it is just as wrong to assume that all railway photographers behave in the same way as it is to assume that all railwaymen are the same.

***Below:*** **Past the goods shed and cattle dock at Maiden Newton comes '14xx' 0-4-2T No 1418 on an auto-train for Weymouth in August 1957.**
*E. Wilmshurst*

# Trains to Whitby

## Martin Bairstow

THE NORTH YORKSHIRE seaside town of Whitby has never enjoyed more than branch line status for its train services. Perhaps its most dramatic contribution to railway history came when it hosted a chance meeting in 1834 between the engineer George Stephenson and the entrepreneur George Hudson. The friendship which built up between the two Georges was of paramount importance in establishing the shape of a substantial proportion of the British railway network.

The next occasion when Whitby's railways hit the national headlines was in the general election campaign of 1964. Harold Wilson gave what many people took to be a pretty definite pledge not to close any of the resort's rail links. The onslaught of Beeching closures was then at its height and the threat to all three lines serving Whitby was regarded as among the more savage proposals which would test any commitment by the incoming Labour Government to amend the policy of the previous administration.

Whitby introduced the 'Railway King' to the 'Father of Railways' and proved that Labour is no more committed to the railway industry than is the Conservative Party. It was also the focal point of a network of scenic and heavily engineered lines whose story dates back almost to the beginning of railways.

George Stephenson was actually there on business in 1834, having been instructed to engineer the Whitby & Pickering Railway. This was brought into use as far as Grosmont in June 1835 and was

***Below:*** **Whitby, 25 August 1980. Class 47 No 47.298 with the stock of an excursion train.** *Peter Harris*

formally opened through to Pickering on 26 May 1836. Between Beck Hole and Bank Top there was a rope-worked incline. The rest of the line was operated by horses. Initially, this line was not connected to any other railway. Indeed, there were very few lines open at that stage. The benefits of railway communication had been brought to Whitby so early because of the physical difficulty of transporting goods inland from the port. There had been a proposal to build a line through the Esk Valley to connect with the Stockton & Darlington, but the consensus of opinion, including that of George Stephenson, was that such a line could offer little advantage over coastal shipping. The line to Pickering would carry goods through the North Yorkshire moors where road transport was very difficult. Beyond Pickering the land is virtually flat by comparison, so a railhead there would be widely accessible.

Meanwhile, rapid progress was being made in establishing a national railway system. On 1 July 1840, the first train reached York by courtesy of the York & North Midland Railway, an undertaking controlled by Hudson, and this connected at Normanton with lines to Manchester, the Midlands and London. The Y&NMR, which was to become part of the North Eastern Railway in 1854, opened the York to Scarborough line and the branch to Pickering on 7 July 1845, one year and three days after gaining Parliamentary approval. At the same time it took over the Whitby & Pickering Railway and started to rebuild this line for locomotive working. The work was completed in 1847 but the incline continued to be rope-worked until 1865. On 1 July of that year, a 4½-mile deviation on a 1 in 49 gradient was opened. The old route was abandoned south of Beck Hole but that hamlet retained a goods service until 1951 and saw a summer-only rail motor for a few years before World War 1.

The North Yorkshire & Cleveland Railway comprised a line through the Esk Valley from Picton to Grosmont. It was opened in sections between 1857 and 1865, by which time it had been incorporated into the NER. Difficult as it may be to imagine nowadays, the rural peace of Glasdale and Grosmont was broken by the operations of ironworks during the last quarter of the nineteenth century, so the Esk Valley was intended as more than just a rural branch line. Iron ore mines in the Rosedale area lead to the construction of a freight-only branch from Battersby which operated from 1861 until 1928 and involved a rope-worked incline. To enable traffic from Rosedale to get direct to Middlesbrough, a branch line was opened in 1864 from Battersby, to connect with the Middlesbrough & Guisborough Railway at Nunthorpe Junction. The branch acquired a passenger service from 1868 but, although authorised, a curve giving direct running from Middlesbrough towards Whitby by avoiding Battersby was never built.

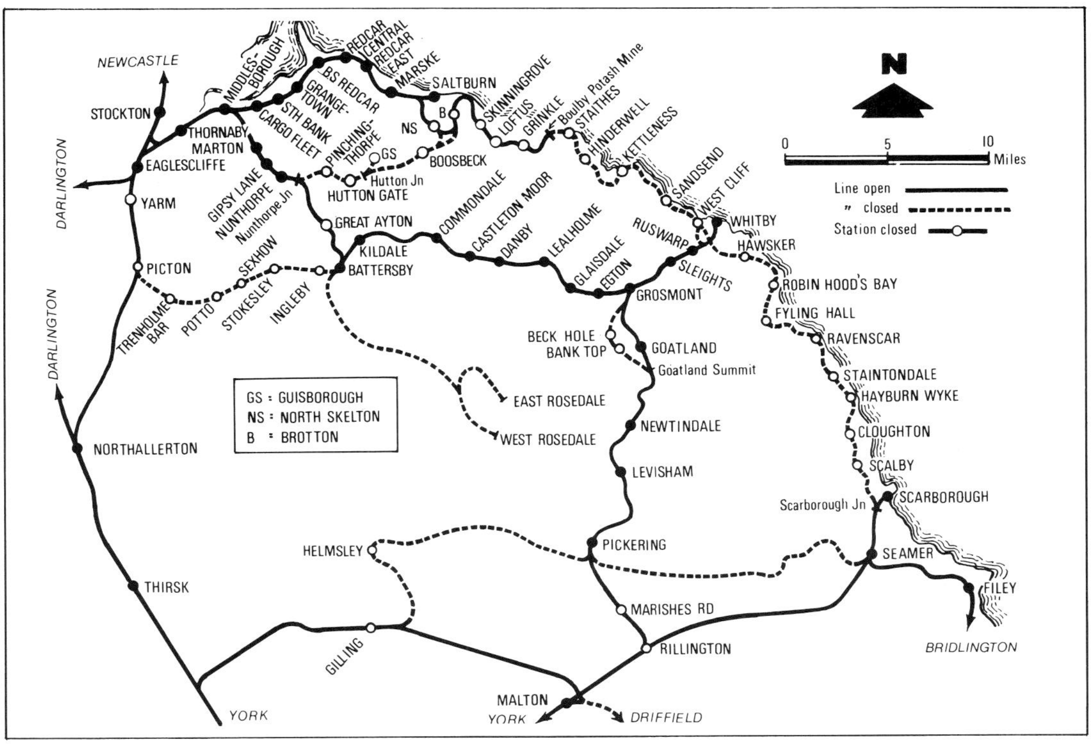

***Above:*** **Vintage appeal at Staithes, 13 July 1957. An Ivatt '4' 2-6-0 crosses the famed viaduct with a Middlesbrough–Whitby train. The viaduct was 152ft in height, with six 60ft and eleven 30ft spans.** *J. C. W. Halliday*

***Right:*** **In steam days, when trains crossed at Battersby, the engines had to run round, too. 'LI' 2-6-4T No 67754 (right) awaits departure for Middlesbrough, as Fairburn 2-6-4T No 42083 runs round its Middlesbrough–Whitby train, 26 April 1958.** *J. C. W. Halliday*

***Below right:*** **The 2.20pm Scarborough–Whitby Town of 15 July 1957 has cleared Ravenscar Tunnel behind 'A8' 4-6-2T No 69867.** *M. Mensing*

***Left:*** **Grosmont on 1 August 1958: Fairburn 2-6-4T No 42085 draws away with the 10.28 am York–Whitby.** *M. Mensing*

The Middlesbrough & Guisborough line, an extension of the Stockton & Darlington Railway, had opened in 1853. Amalgamated with the NER in 1863, it was extended from Hutton Junction, near Guisborough, to Loftus in 1867. An alternative route to Loftus was provided in 1875 when the Saltburn to Brotton link opened. These lines were heavily involved with Teesside industry, but a line along the coast from Loftus to Scarborough would be primarily a passenger facility. The Whitby, Redcar & Middlesbrough Union Railway was authorised in 1866 but, not surprisingly, took rather longer to complete than some of the more commercial lines already mentioned. It was opened on 3 December 1883 and commenced at a junction with the Whitby & Pickering line at Bog Hall. In the 16½ miles to Loftus the line crossed five major viaducts, passed through two tunnels and was very close to the sea for much of the way.

Meanwhile, the Scarborough & Whitby Railway was making similar progress, finally opening on 16 July 1885, from Falsgrave Junction, Scarborough, to Prospect Hill Junction near Whitby, which it reached by the 13-arch Esk Viaduct. The gradients were severe, the summit at Ravenscar being attained by a two-mile climb at 1 in 41 from the south, and almost three miles at 1 in 39 from Fyling Hall.

For many years the main passenger service ran from Saltburn to Scarborough. The trains had to 'set back' to gain access to both termini. A frequent local service provided connections at West Cliff to and from Whitby. In 1933, the pattern was changed with the Scarborough trains running from Middlesbrough via Nunthorpe. The summer timetable in 1938 provided 15 trains from West Cliff to Middlesbrough and a similar number to Scarborough, the majority being fed by a Sentinel steam railcar connecting from Whitby Town at West Cliff. On the Pickering line at this time there were 11 advertised trains, but that number was heavily augmented by excursions. Five trains ran to Stockton via Picton affording connections at Battersby for Middlesbrough. The Sentinel railcars managed six return journeys from Whitby to Goathland and five to Glaisdale.

The early 1950s saw the closure of some of the less used lines. The Saltburn to Brotton passenger service succumbed in 1951. The Battersby to Picton line closed in 1954, after which all Esk Valley trains had to reverse to reach Middlesbrough via Nunthorpe. Far more significant was the running of the last train from Middlesbrough to Scarborough by the coast route on 3 May 1958. Closure between Loftus and Whitby West Cliff was blamed on the cost of maintaining the viaducts, but retraction was not without its compensations. The following Monday an improved timetable commenced via Battersby giving the Esk Valley line a better service than ever before, as well as introducing diesel multiple-units which made light work of the four reversals at Battersby, Whitby Town, West Cliff and outside Scarborough. A dmu service continued mainly at peak-hours between Middlesbrough and Loftus, but was cut back to Guisborough in May 1960, and to Nunthorpe in March 1964. Whitby West Cliff station closed on 10 June 1961, after which Scarborough trains reversed at Prospect Hill Junction.

When Dr Beeching came to publish his report in 1963, Whitby still enjoyed a good rail access from three directions. Those of us who believe in railway development would acknowledge that some rationalisation of the BR network of the time was not only inevitable, but highly desirable. Few would really argue with the concentration on one route north of Whitby as achieved in 1958. The two southern routes were less directly in competition with one another, but sensible rationalisation could perhaps have dispensed with one of them. If the prime object had been to retain good access to Whitby from the rest of the system, then the route from York via Pickering was the obvious choice. The alternative of running trains via Scarborough would have been slower, but would have served the smaller resorts such as Robin Hoods Bay. The attractiveness of the Scarborough – Middlesborough service could then have been enhanced by closing some of the least-used stations, turning the junction at Battersby the other way (this was the one reversal caused by historical accident rather than topography) and running trains through to the main line railhead at Darlington.

The Beeching proposals involved not merely rationalisation, but the complete elimination of railways from an area of the country where the economy was heavily dependent on tourism and where a number of communities were without other public transport. The practicalities of substituting bus services could have appealed only to somebody who had never visited the area. Any adequate substitute would have required separate local and long-distance buses and probably new roads for them to run on. The main road between Malton and Whitby does not pass through either Goathland or Grosmont, so that a through bus must either miss them out or take a lengthy detour.

The proposal to close all three lines was put to the Transport Users' Consultative Committee who reported that 'serious hardship' would result from withdrawal of any of the passenger services. In September 1964, Ernest Marples, Minister of Transport and political architect of the Beeching policy, pronounced judgement. Especially in view of an imminent general election something more favourable had been expected than the decision that only the Middlesbrough line would be reprieved.

The Esk Valley certainly contained its share of otherwise isolated intermediate villages and a good proportion of Whitby's holiday traffic undoubtedly came from the north-east, but the Middlesbrough-Whitby line hardly provided an adequate rail link with other parts of the country. In response to questions in the House, the new Labour Minister of Transport said that he could not vary a decision made by his predecessor. Then followed the customary threats of that time to raise private capital to take over the lines, or have them subsidised out of the rates and the local MP attempted to introduce a Private Member's Bill to force BR to keep them open. None of this interferred with the planned closure date, and on Saturday, 6 March 1965 the last ordinary trains were joined by a 'Whitby Moors Rail Tour' hauled by Gresley 'K4' 2-6-0 No 3442 *The Great Marquess* and 'K1' 2-6-0 No 62005 (now on the North Yorkshire Moors Railway.)

For a few years, the BR timetables listed Whitby as 'a place not directly served by rail' while the Leeds – Scarborough table showed bus connections for Whitby, together with a note that 'bus times were not available at the time of going to press'. This attempt at road-rail co-ordination was short-lived.

***Below:*** **In 1978, the former North Eastern Railway water column at Battersby was repainted, but its services are not required by this Whitby-bound diesel multiple-unit.** *Rodney Wildsmith*

***Below right:*** **The North Yorkshire Moors Railway boasts ex-Western Region diesel hydraulic locomotives, such as No D7029 seen at Thomason Force with the 13.55 Grosmont–Pickering on 13 July 1982.** *W. A. Sharman*

Outside the north-east, BR has almost denied Whitby's rail links since 1965.

By June 1967, the tracks south of Whitby were about to be lifted when a small group of people got together to discuss the possibility of forming a society to preserve part of one line. One condition at the time of closure was that the track would be left in place, at least temporarily. The result was the formation of the North Yorkshire Moors Railway Preservation Society with the object of restoring services from Grosmont for six miles, as far as Goathland Summit. There it was envisaged that a terminus would be established at the point where the Lyke Wake Walk crosses the line. Negotiations with BR revealed that the 12 miles of trackbed thence to Pickering were available at a relatively low cost so the opportunity was taken to secure this section.

The North Riding (later North Yorkshire) County Council supported the preservation scheme in view of the tourist potential of the line through Newtondale and so purchased the track from Goathland Summit to Pickering for lease back to the Railway. This enabled the full 18 miles to reopen in April 1973. Initially, steam trains operated between Grosmont and Goathland, with just a sparse dmu service thence to Pickering. The task of maintaning and operating a line three times the length originally envisaged has put an enormous strain upon a voluntary organisation. Fortunately, the volume of traffic – and particularly that originating from Pickering – appears to have justified the decision to go for the longer line. The NYMR has certainly experienced problems associated with under-capitalisation, the mixing of full-time staff with volunteers and the practical difficulties of accommodating the volume of traffic on offer. During 1982, the Railway operated every day from 1 April to 31 October with roughly half the trains scheduled for steam haulage and the remainder for an expanding fleet of preserved diesel classes or dmus. This level of service is the most comprehensive provided by a standard gauge preserved railway. As with other preserved lines, the overwhelming majority of the passengers are tourists, but in the case of the NYMR it would seem that they are attracted as much by the scenery as by the operation of steam locomotives. The NYMR is nonetheless committed to maintaining a steam locomotive fleet which includes ex-NER and LNER classes not represented anywhere else.

Despite the loss of the Scarborough passengers and helped a little by the NYMR, Esk Valley passenger traffic has held up well since 1965. Timetable improvements in 1976 included the provision of a commuter service as far as Nunthorpe with an additional station at Gypsy Lane. Since May 1982, nearly all Whitby line trains have started from Darlington and, thanks to the Inter-City 125s, the overall journey time from King's Cross to Whitby is on occasions less than it was before closure of the Pickering route – something which BR might exploit.

Freight on the Esk Valley line is minimal, though at one time it looked as though major flows would be generated by a proposed potash mine near Hawsker, on the Whitby-Scarborough section. With this in mind, the track between Whitby and Hawsker was left in situ for some years after closure. Ironically enough, the environmental lobby, while claiming to support rail transport, fiercely opposed a scheme which would provide local employment, secure the future of the Esk Valley line and still leave 99% of the moors unspoilt.

Further north at Boulby an application to sink a potash mine was more successful. This led to the reinstatement of four miles of railway from Skinningrove where the ironworks had ensured the survival of a freight service from Saltburn Junction.

Something certainly remains of the interesting railway system in this area and the reader is recommended to take advantage of the through bookings which are available from Middlesbrough to Pickering. Having traversed 47 steeply graded and sharply curved miles through splendid scenery he will note that he is only 6½ miles from the York – Scarborough line at Rillington. This section, last used for goods in July 1966, was an easily graded line through flat country. The formation has now been redeveloped in Pickering.

# Steam in the docks

## D. Trevor Rowe

INDUSTRIAL enthusiasts of the 1950s and 1960s were able to find steam locomotives in use in a wide variety of industries, collieries being a prime example. Cement works, the iron and steel industry and paper mills all added to the scene with oddities such as Aveling Porter geared locomotives and fireless types.

Port authorities were generally conservative and used mainly standard 0-6-0 and 0-4-0 tank engines, but there were often large fleets working over extensive systems. This feature illustrates a few of these machines, in service with organisations such as the Port of London Authority, the Port of Bristol Authority and the Mersey Docks and Harbour Board. Others will spring readily to the mind of the older enthusiast, in particular the Manchester Ship Canal Railway, the Seaham Harbour system, and Par Harbour in the far west. Such systems lacked the scenic attractions of the Welsh coal railways, or the ironstone quarries in the East Midlands, although they might be considered more photogenic than the average gasworks system.

The Port of London Authority was formed in 1909 from several earlier dock companies and latterly had locomotive depots at Millwall, Custom House (for the Royal group of docks), West India Docks (worked from Millwall by the late 1950s) and Tilbury. By the late 1950s, a reasonably standardised fleet had replaced the earlier types and all were 0-4-0 or 0-6-0 tank engines, which could look very smart in lined-out blue livery. Although all the locomotives illustrated happen to have been built by Hudswell Clarke, other builders were represented, with Hawthorn Leslie and Peckett in a minority. Many of the ex-War Department Austerities came from Hunslet and Robert

**Port of London Authority steam shunters in October 1957:**

***Top right:*** **No 89, Hudswell Clarke 0-4-0ST, (Works No 1875/53).**

***Centre right:*** **No 45, Hudswell Clarke 0-6-0T, (Works No 1101/15).**

***Bottom right:*** **No 80, an Austerity 0-6-0ST, built by Hudswell Clarke in 1943 for the War Department.**

Stephenson and Hawthorns. Diesels first made their appearance at Tilbury in the shape of six Yorkshire Engine Company 0-6-0 diesel electrics in 1956/57.

At Liverpool, the Mersey Docks and Harbour Board had a fleet of 0-6-0STs, built by Avonside and Hunslet at various dates between 1904 and 1941. There was also a fireless locomotive built by Andrew Barclay in 1914. The first diesel had arrived in 1944 and a batch came from Hudswell Clarke in 1958.

The Port of Bristol Authority had depots in two counties, the principal one being at Avonmouth Docks, Gloucestershire. By the 1950s, the steam stock consisted entirely of 0-6-0STs from Peckett and Avonside, dating from 1900 to 1943. All were named. The first diesel came in 1950, and was soon followed by others from Hudswell Clarke, all named in the tradition of the steam fleet. At Portishead Docks in Somerset, a Peckett 0-6-0ST dating from 1904 was paired with a Hudswell Clarke 0-4-0 diesel, although transfers to and from Avonmouth were often made as required.

***Top left:*** **Mersey Docks & Harbour Board: No 11, a standard-type Hunslet 0-6-0ST (HE 1985/40). In the background is a locomotive employed by contractors dismantling the Liverpool Overhead Railway.**

***Left:*** **The Port of Bristol Authority: at Avonmouth stands No S13 *Redland,* an 0-6-0ST, Peckett's No 2038 of 1943, and seen in August 1960.**

***Below:*** **Steam and diesel in service at Avonmouth shed, in August 1960.** *All photographs D. Trevor Rowe*

# Departing images

To conclude . . . a look at the way in which different photographers have captured the scene of trains arriving, departing and passing . . .

***Left:*** **At least two passengers at New Eltham seem oblivious to the arrival of a Dartford–Sidcup–Charing Cross train in March 1981.** *Brian Morrison*

***Below:*** **More to the eye . . . The guard of the 16.53 Paddington–Exeter waves away his train at Newbury while behind him has crept up an empty diesel unit to form a train to Bedwyn. July 1979.**
*D. E. Canning*

***Right:*** **Western Region atmosphere, early 1960s. We'll leave you to guess where!** *D. Anderson*

***Below right:*** **A Class 101 dmu out-smokes 'West Country' 4-6-2 No 34092 *City of Wells* standing outside Leeds City on 10 August 1982.**
*Dr John Sagar*

***Right:*** **More to the eye . . . Look closely and the overbridge is clearly swarming with photographers, intent on recording Stirling Single No 1 between Loughborough and Rothley, 6 December 1981.** *J. H. Cooper-Smith*

***Below: Evening Star,*** **Abergavenny, 24 April 1982.** *Dave Hunt*